Datacenter Migration using the ROPE Framework
Results Oriented Project Execution

Rhythm of
the business

Future of
technology

24

Keep the
lights on

PMO
Governance

Datacenter Migration using the ROPE Framework

Results Oriented Project Execution

Written by Paul Thompson

Published by Metagyre, Inc.

2019

Intelligent project execution for a complex technology world.

First Printing: 2019

ISBN 978-0-359-46297-1

Metagyre, Inc.
1249 NW Arcadia Ct, Suite 300
Poulsbo, WA. 98370

www.metagyre.com

This book is dedicated to the most gifted team of individuals I've ever had the privilege to work alongside. Their skills raised the bar and they demonstrated on a daily basis how to consistently achieve positive results. Without their inspiration, poking and prodding this guide would never have been completed.

Karen Grose who always had may back and provided the sounding board for the concepts in this guide. Tim Adamsen for support with the hard stuff and instilling in me that on-time is late. Marc Swenson who always took on the tasks no one else wanted and came back with a smile.

Table of Contents

Preface

This is a practical guide to applying the ROPE framework to a datacenter migration project. This guide is intended for executive leaders, PMO (project management office) leaders, program managers, project managers or others interested in understanding how to successfully build out a datacenter and migrate applications without negatively impacting their business.

Over the years it has become clear there is no standard datacenter migration project. Some datacenter migration projects involve building a new facility and migrating applications into a green field technology stack. Other datacenter migration projects involve moving into existing datacenter space, taking advantage of current resource capacity for the application migration. Then of course, there are migration projects all along the spectrum.

When we developed the ROPE (results-oriented project execution) framework and applied it to a datacenter migration, the goal was for it to have enough structure to ensure success while retaining the flexibility needed for different forms of complex technology projects, all the while minimizing business impacts. After a decade of migrating datacenters and leading numerous complex technology initiatives for various organizations, we believe we achieved our goal with this framework. This belief comes from not only our success, but also having many customers adopt the ROPE framework as the standard for running all their complex technology projects.

From the beginning, a driving force in the development of the ROPE framework has been a customer focus that would mesh a datacenter migrations' workflow into the rhythm of the business. Every business function or department has a rhythm to its workflow. By tying technology changes into the rhythm of the business, we acknowledge the business knows better than anyone when they can absorb change. Sliding small sized technical work packages into the ebb and flow of the business minimizes disruption and maximizes results.

The other major guiding principle in developing the ROPE framework were:

- Deliver continual, incremental value to the business.
- Welcome diversity, control change, manage scope.
- Face-to-face conversations are most effective at resolving roadblocks.
- Teams are more powerful than any individual.
- Over optimization of a project's subparts slows down throughput of the whole project.
- Single piece work is the ideal.
- Codify lessons and apply them quickly.
- Elegant solutions are usually the simplest.

A final input to developing the ROPE framework was the acceptance that with complex technology projects it is impossible to know every requirement and freeze them before you begin to execute on the next step of a plan.

Complex technology projects such as a datacenter migration are filled with ambiguity, uncertainty and risk. This ambiguity can be overwhelming initially. The framework's road map acknowledges this uncertainty, embraces what is known, learns as it goes and incrementally builds to a stable, repeatable, deployment method that is predictable, sustainable and positively impacts the business.

Datacenter Migration Road Map

Multiple work streams on parallel paths come together for a successful datacenter migration

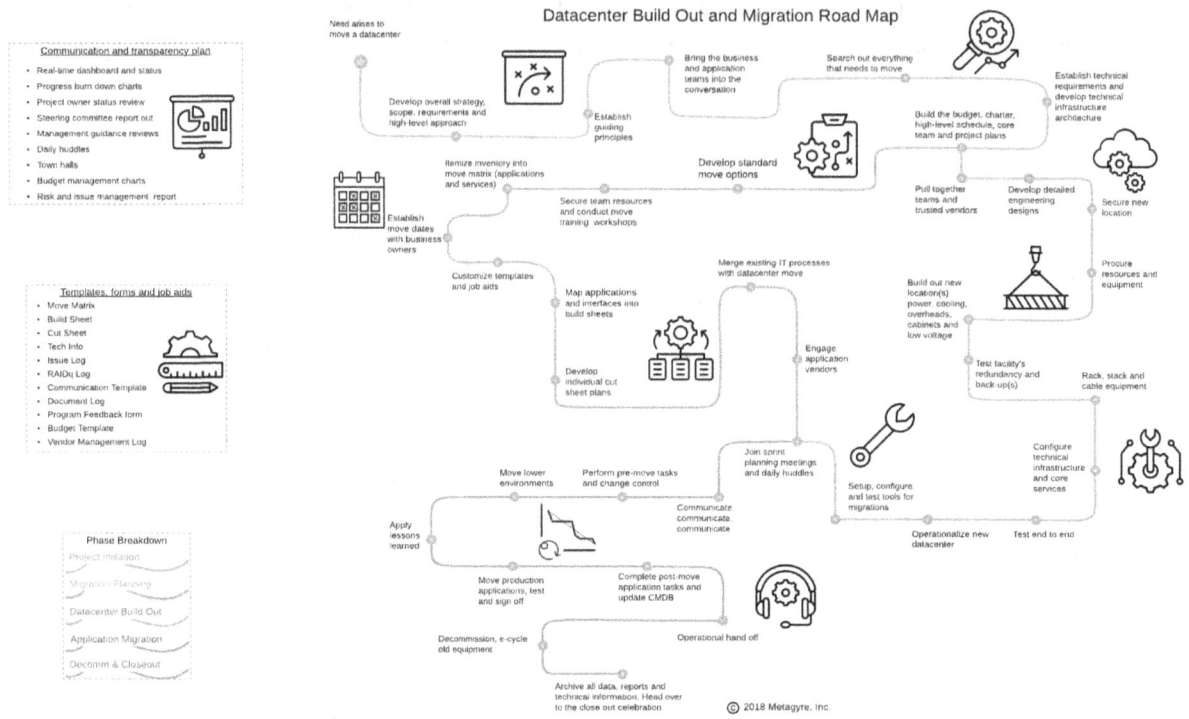

As you read through this guide, we hope you will see how the ROPE framework fits into your specific organization's datacenter migration project. It is important to understand that this guide presents a successful framework, not an absolute step by step measured out recipe. Every datacenter migration project will need to tailor these framework items slightly to fit into the organization's culture and changing business drivers.

We have witnessed this framework successfully execute datacenter migrations and many other complex technology projects. The ROPE framework is solid, but it is not a guarantee. Organizations with a culture that is uncomfortable with change and does not trust their staff to make good decisions, will have challenges accepting an approach that admits to gathering information all along the way and takes advantage of small batch sizes to shorten the cycle times of applying lessons learned.

If your organization falls into a more waterfall-oriented culture, you may want to utilize the ROPE framework components and layer work-breakdowns and Gantt charts on top. In our view this adds additional, unnecessary work, but it may be the only way deal with cultural deadlock.

Leadership

As you start down the path of your datacenter migration using the ROPE framework, some individuals throughout the organization will start to feel uncomfortable. Organizations accustomed to following a traditional waterfall approach may feel insecure about proceeding on a path that does not have the traditional road signs they are familiar with, such as a detailed Gantt chart, critical path analysis, frozen requirements, or traditional dependency diagrams.

Across most of our customers, we have experienced this situation of uneasiness to varying degrees. The recommended solution to this organizational vibration is to deliver the training program as early and to as many stakeholders as possible and for leadership to assure individuals that this is the framework and method the organization has committed to using for this datacenter migration. The message is for everyone to lean in and trust in the process. In some organizations this reassurance may need to come from the very top in order to provide the calming affect required to work through the ambiguity and mistrust that comes with change.

Senior leadership

Purpose: Consistent priority and communication that amplifies program importance, maintains scope and fosters ownership. Instill the sense of urgency across the enterprise.

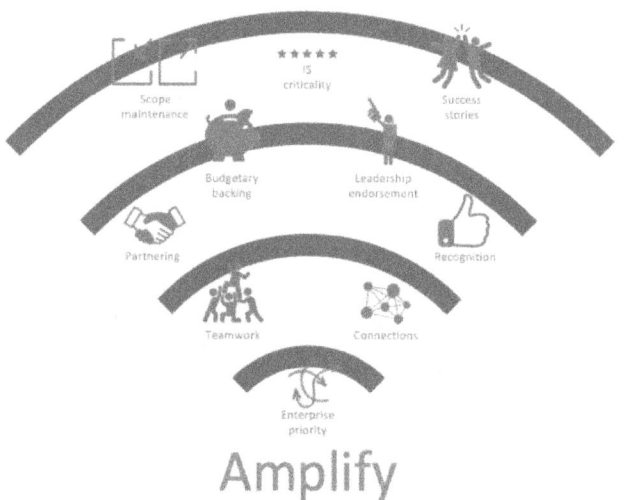

Amplify

Organizations who already practice a more agile methodology will recognize many of the ROPE framework's components and quickly adapt to the subtle differences and data requirements. Regardless of an organization's ability to work with the ROPE framework, senior leadership's ability to amplify the message of importance and project priority will affect the final outcome.

However you choose to move your datacenter or whomever you bring in to lead the datacenter migration, one point must be clear: an organization cannot outsource accountability for the datacenter move. The leaders of the organization must understand that the final outcome and the ease or difficulty of the migration is ultimately owned by the organization and not the project management team. As a leadership team, it is important to make an informed decision about how the datacenter migration project will be organized and run, then ensure the enterprise as a whole understands their role. Without visible top leadership support, completing the datacenter migration with the desired results will be difficult.

The Secret Sauce

The secret is that there really is no secret. Reliable project execution is the result of hard work, planning, communication and commitment. The ROPE framework uses common sense methods and tools to direct the planning, focus work, provide transparency and gain commitments from those involved without adding undue overhead or unnecessary processes.

ROPE stands for Results Oriented Project Execution. In order to deliver on this promise there are some simple tenets that drive the framework. Those tenets are:

- Actively involve the business in every way.
- Deliver continual, incremental value to the business.
- Welcome diversity, control change and manage scope.
- Senior leadership actively supports the project.
- Provide guiding principles that allow decisions to be made by those closest to the issue.
- Organize and present tasks in a way that is clear to those performing the work not those managing the work.
- Teamwork is required to untie big, ugly, hairy technology knots. The right people working together will solve the unsolvable.
- Simplicity is elegant, avoid over-engineering around a roadblock.
- Face issues, problems and roadblocks head on.
- Talking is the best form of communication. Choose interactive digital communication methods second and email as a last resort.
- Every project work flow has constraints.
    1. Identify the project work flow bottle neck.
    2. Exploit the bottle neck by making it as efficient as possible.
    3. Let the bottle neck drive the pace.
    4. Look at additional resources or purchases to remove the bottle neck.
    5. The constraint will move in the work flow once the original bottle neck is resolved, go to step 1.
- Remove unnecessary work where ever possible. Reduce work in process (WIP) making throughput a top priority.
- Don't allow everything to become a snowflake. Develop efficient repeatable project workflows and stick to it.
- Codify lessons and apply them quickly to improve each iteration within the project.

As you will see throughout this guide on moving a datacenter, using the ROPE framework, the tenets above drive the way tasks are managed, how activities are performed and who is involved in achieving the desired results.

The ultimate secret to successfully executing complex technology projects is for an organization to honestly know itself.

Organizations who align with the tenet behind the ROPE framework will find numerous applications for ROPE and quickly see the results they are working toward.

On the other hand, if an organization has a track record of fighting change, missing commitments and working in silos with a shortage of leadership support, no methodology or framework is going to immediately turn around results.   However, if leadership is committed to changing behaviors and actively involved in the ROPE framework even the most difficult cultural situations can be turned around. Make no mistake about it, cultural change is hard work.

Scope, Death By 1,000 Cuts

Scope for a datacenter migration project may seem straight forward. If it is in the old datacenter, move it into the new datacenter. Inevitably identifying scope is harder than this. When starting up a new datacenter move project one of the most important items is establishing what is in scope and more importantly what is out of scope.

The number one reason a datacenter migration project goes sideways is what we refer to as "death by 1,000 cuts". These are all the little and sometimes not so little, items that get tacked onto the project. For example:

- All servers will be upgraded to the new OS standard.
- SQL databases will be upgraded to the newest SQL Server cluster.
- DR plan upgrades will be implemented and tested as applications are moved.
- The current flat network architecture will be replaced with an application centric infrastructure, incorporating a complete set of policy driven security controls.
- Application re-platforming to take advantage of lower software upgrade costs.
- Application rationalization of redundant and outdated systems.
- New controls will be installed and activated to remediate compliance exceptions.
- Application upgrades for applications deemed Tier 1 or 2.
- New Active Directory domain for applications in the new datacenter.
- The list goes on...

Some of the cuts are necessary. Old underlying equipment needs to be replaced. Network and compute architectures need to be brought forward to industry standard. Storage platforms must accommodate the need for faster access of more data.

The difficulty for many organizations is striking the balance between setting an achievable design change that provides for the future and the desire to pay back all technical debt accumulated over the past decade.

One way to recognize where the line of demarcation should be set is to look at impact and repeatability. For example, upgrading the virtual compute systems to a fully converged architecture is a large change. But that change should only be a single event. Once the new platform is in place and provisioning is brought on line, deploying new or receiving migrated virtual servers is a repeatable and predictable process. On the other hand, upgrading operating systems means that each of the hundreds of applications needs to be compatible, supported, upgraded, tested and remediated on the new OS. Each application will be different, having different issues associated with the upgrade, requiring different solutions.

While changing out the underlying platform architecture may seem like a deeper cut than an application upgrade, in the context of a datacenter move, the architecture change is much more manageable provided operational readiness and effective supporting structures around the new architecture can be put in place.

In general changes that affect an application are significantly riskier than changes that are limited to the underlying infrastructure. In other words, you can install new firewalls and segment the network VLANs into different zones minimally affecting the applications, but requiring new firewall rules for each application to traverse the various VLANs has a significant impact on scheduling and increases the risk of encountering unpredictable results.

Throughout this guide we use the term "Like for Like" to indicate you should not be changing anything that doesn't absolutely have to change. Even though most of the time an individual change will seem small, multiplied by the number of applications and services to move, small changes become death by 1,000 cuts.

Unseen Scope

Most clients who approach us with a datacenter migration project have a reasonable handle on the number of applications needing to move to the new datacenter. Many times, they have sized the application according to small, medium, large or simple, medium, complex. Most have missed a large chunk of the effort.

Few clients consider the infrastructure services as a part of this count. Infrastructure services include everything from Active Directory (AD), domain name services (DNS), dynamic host configuration protocol (DHCP), circuit moves and virtual private network (VPN) access to network tunnels as well as load balanced virtual IP (VIP) addresses and all the other services supporting applications. In some cases, the scope increase can be as much as half depending on how services are defined within an organization.

Identifying all the infrastructure services is an important part of the scope count. As a part of moving the service, it is critical to identify what is affected when the service is migrated. Identifying affected items using a service can prove extremely difficult. Many times, the team supporting an infrastructure service such as a GRE (generic routine encapsulation) Tunnel, has no visibility into how the service is used, the applications accessed or the impact of downtime. The impacts of moving infrastructure services without knowing who or how it is used can be catastrophic in the case of clinical healthcare, plant operation, or other critical 24x7 systems. The effort involved in service moves is significant and involves staff from several areas as well as customer and vendor/partner personnel.

The other scope issue with service migrations involves changing platforms, architecture or technology improvement. An example of this can be seen moving from an outdated Cisco firewall to a next generation Palo Alto, Cisco, or other manufacturer's firewall. Most likely, the old firewall rules will be a mess, poorly documented and filled with legacy objects no longer used. While there are tools to help, there is no silver bullet to unraveling legacy chaos. The reality is that service migrations are significant work.

A key to managing this unseen scope is to consider infrastructure services the same as an application. Services will move a bit different than an application, but they should be identified, tracked, managed and staffed like any other application.

Scheduling and Time-line

As you will see throughout this guide, we don't typically create a traditional Gantt based schedule. Instead we attempt to back into the scheduling starting with leadership's desired end date as the target completion.

This approach is important because we find that senior leadership is considering information seldom known by the majority of the staff such as upcoming mergers, major strategic business shifts and other high impact events to the enterprise. This does not mean the project can guarantee a completion by the target date, but it does provide a starting point.

HIGH-LEVEL TIME-LINE
How soon do we have to get started and when are we done

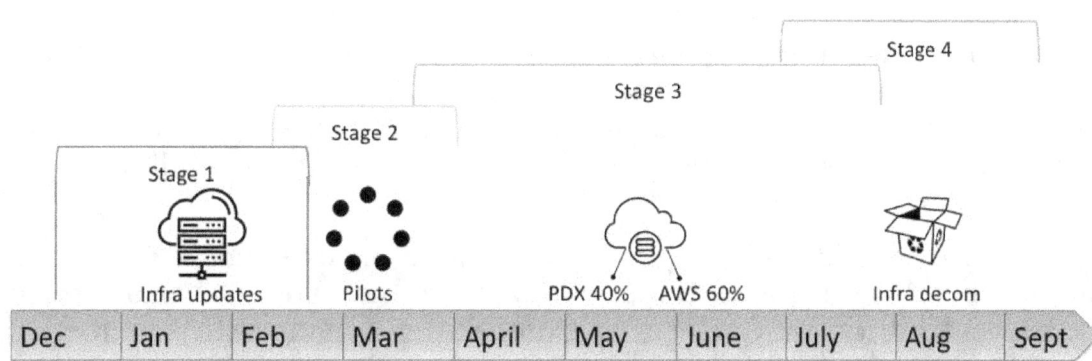

With a target end date in hand, assemble the project management team along with key technical and application leaders to time box the four main stages of the project along a time line. At this point you are looking to establish boundaries in order to time box major activities and convey a sense of pace at which the project is going to have to achieve and maintain over the entire project. As the managers pull together their time boxes, ensure they consider options for staff augmentation and resetting other priorities in order to meet leadership's target end date.

Start by determining how long it will take to procure and complete the build out of the new datacenter. This phase should include developing the IT infrastructure design, procuring equipment and deploying it into a fully ready datacenter space. Don't under estimate the time required to:

- Select a site and negotiate contracts.
- Design cabinet layouts and structure cabling.

- Integrate designs across all engineering disciplines.
- Procure and receive all the equipment desired.
- Install network circuits.
- Duration to deploy, configure and test the IT equipment individually and as a complete set of systems.

The infrastructure build typically takes longer than management anticipates with early activities such as site selection, contract negation and procurement extending well beyond original estimates.

The pilot stage is typically five to eight weeks. This time allows teams to:

- Move their first set of low priority applications.
- Infrastructure teams complete any lagging build out such as DMZ.
- Identify and codify lessons to future moves

During the pilot phase you will be proving out several items in the overall approach plan as well as ensuring everyone is comfortable with their role in the move event. Don't anticipate much reduction in this phase. In fact, if you have not fully engaged the supporting groups such as DBAs and engineers the pilot may have to refine a good deal of steps. Additionally, if application analysts and business customers have not put in the effort to develop solid build sheets and cut sheets, the throughput in the pilot phase will be significantly slower than desired.

Unless you are contractually required to evacuate the existing datacenter, the decommission phase can be addressed at a pace that allows other projects to gain a higher priority for engineers and datacenter options team members since the primary goal of the project, to exit the current datacenter, is complete. The decommission phase can be lengthy depending on the desired end results. When time boxing this phase consider what is in scope.

- Return the space to original office space.
- Convert from a datacenter to a network MDF.
- Maintain as a datacenter form DR, Dev/Test environments and infrastructure lab.

When estimating time, remember you will most likely be scheduling several subcontractors to perform work. This includes e-cyclers to remove equipment, storage vendors to wipe disks clean and reclaim equipment, vendors to remove or reroute structured cabling, facility contractors to terminate electrical connections, remove chillers and cap water pipes, ... With this much interdependency among external vendors it is easy for schedules to slip.

The last phase to estimate is the application move phase. On large datacenter migrations we have found planned velocity to be an effective estimating tool. You can gain a reasonable estimate by multiplying the number of items by the desired velocity. For example, if you have 100 applications and want a velocity of 1, it will take you 100 calendar days to complete the migration phase. While simple, we have found that this estimating technique works quiet well for most organizations. Of course, there are some caveats to this approach.

- A planned velocity between .5 and 1.5 is usually achievable but your organization's ability to prioritize work, maintain focus, accept risk and deal with change will affect results.
- Consider that a velocity of 1 is the same as moving one application a day, every day without a break for the duration of the phase. While this is not the actual way it will unfold, it does put into perspective the amount of work a velocity of 1 involves. If this is your first datacenter migration, consider using a velocity of between .5 and .75 to set your timebox.
- If you are extending your network's layer 2, keeping IP addresses and host names the same and you plan to perform live moves of the workloads, consider applications running on virtual servers separately. Most compute teams can move between 200 to 250 virtual servers each week if you have available hardware capacity in the new datacenter.
- Physical moves are inevitable. Plan for multiple small truck loads rather than one or two large truck loads. Include the time required to ensure the new location is ready to accept the physical devices. This includes pre-cabling, rail installs, data copies, network and SAN port setups, as well as any ancillary service needs such as POTs lines, or VIPs, or firewall rule changes. As an example: one of our clients successfully moved 200 physical devices (servers, blades, chassis, network devices, storage, ...) over a 30-day time frame in ten move events. Another client took three months to move the equivalent number of items.

Now place the four phases end to end and see how they align to leadership's original target. There will be some natural overlap with the phases. However, if you are aggressively removing all the slack in your plan at the start by overlapping your phases, you should expect to readdress and adjust the end date several times along the way.

Once you have the phases time boxed you can start to drive the teams to these dates as you develop the move matrix and build out matrix. Remember these dates are targets. If you and your leadership team have been realistic about your enterprise's capabilities, you should be able to execute to these dates and deliver. Throughout the project you will be continuously evaluating your burn downs to see if you are staying on your planned velocity. If it becomes clear you have set the target dates too aggressively, the leadership team will need to consider adding staff, reducing scope or extending the date.

Later, this guide will discuss building your projects details and individual move dates. For now, feel confident you have solid milestones that can be used to time box the tasks within those phases and that teams have a high-level understanding of what they need to execute against.

Results Oriented Project Execution (ROPE) Framework

Agile projects have a lot of benefits: an incremental approach, the ability to change direction based on business drivers and stakeholder feedback, short timeframes that keeps teams focused. We use the term "agile", but it would be just as appropriate to link the ROPE framework's methods to "Lean Manufacturing", "Scrum" or even underlying principles of "DevOps". Agile is a mindset of radical transparency and admitting that the team doesn't know all the answers at the beginning of a project, which can be difficult at first for some to accept.

Our ROPE framework has four basic parts with the "Move Train" being the most agile oriented set of activities. However, the entire framework is built on the understanding that the project will need to be in a continual learning mode since you will never have all the information documented or calibrated from the start. Using the concept of a rolling wave, where tasks and items become more clearly defined as they approach, the framework establishes guidelines and practices that if followed will draw in the information as it is needed, preventing teams from getting stuck in analysis paralysis.

The goal throughout the framework is to optimize for overall throughput. Lean has shown that the best way to improve throughput, is to reduce work batch sizes. In applying the ROPE framework to datacenter migrations, we aim for single application batch sizes.

ROPE Framework

The results oriented project execution framework is a flexible, iterative approach that minimizes business stress, maintains schedule momentum and delivers success without loosing visibility, quality or control.

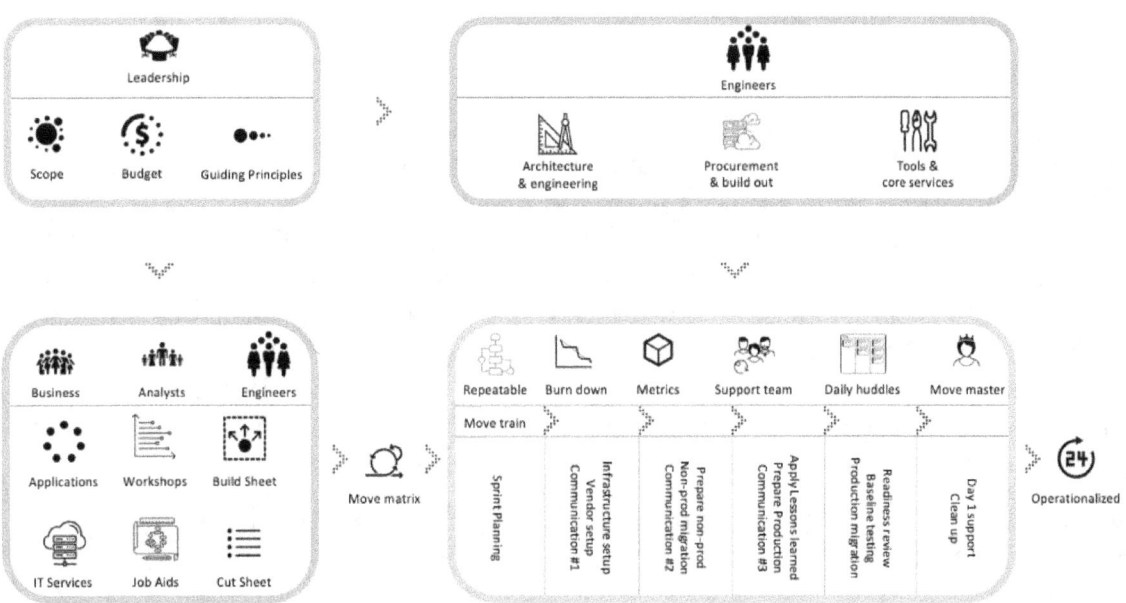

As you can see in the diagram above, the four parts to the ROPE framework are "Leadership Guidance", "Engineering Build", "Discovery Planning" and "Move Train".

Leadership Guidance

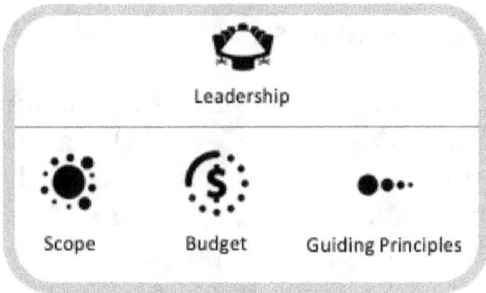

The guidance received from leadership is crucial to the success of a datacenter migration or other complex technology project. In order to be successful, this guidance needs to be a collaborative effort between leadership and the project management team. Skipping or glossing over this step can lead to needless difficulties throughout the project.

In the ROPE framework, three areas of leadership guidance are stressed. These areas are:

- Scope
- Budget
- Guiding principles

Scope

Scope is generally straight forward, but some points need to be tightly screwed down. A good place to start is with the applications and services. Usually all applications must be moved out of the old datacenter. This is true for most services. In some cases, the old datacenter will remain as a network MDF (main distribution frame) or dev-test environment or to house location specific applications. Applications and services left behind should be identified and noted as out of scope or where the boundary is for those items. At a high-level, this is good to flesh out, just recognize that the actual list of applications in scope will come later and maintained in the move matrix.

Often it is more important to clearly identify what is out of scope. Several examples include:

- Equipment not within the datacenter (aka ancillary data closets, located in other datacenters, under desks).
- Upgrade of operating systems not currently at standard.
- Upgrade of applications.
- Active Directory consolidation.
- Client upgrades not directly related to the movement of applications.
- Operational support processes.
- Database upgrades or changes.
- Application lifecycles activities.
- Disaster recovery improvements.

Be very clear what is not included as a part of the scope in order to avoid scope creep. We refer to scope creep as "death by 1,000 cuts" and it is a significant reason a datacenter migration project goes sideways. It can be difficult to gain initial agreement on scope. Some may want to use the datacenter migration project as a forcing function for teams to pay back their technical debt. Others feel it is more efficient to pay down technical debt during a datacenter move rather than repay the debt prior to or after the applications, service or systems have moved. In our experience, this is seldom true. The additional scope requires far more effort and causes delays beyond original estimates. Changes to applications slow the rate at which an application can migrate from one datacenter to the other, making each move a project unto itself rather than an item on the move train.

This is not to say nothing can ever change, but leadership should be very deliberate with its choices. Changes to individual applications are far more disruptive than changing from a Citrix NetScaler load balancer to an F5 load balancer. The reason for the difference in the impact is that once the changes required to go from NetScaler to F5 are understood and codified they can be repeated for all application moves with little to no impact at the application level. Changes to an individual application require unique design, implementation and testing investments for each application. Applications are far more difficult to change as part of a datacenter move than the underlying infrastructure. However, there is a limit to how much infrastructure can be changed without impacting the engineering staff. This decision will need to be tempered with budget for engineers to train on the new technology as well as additional time for implementation and testing. We recommend vendors of the infrastructure technology be heavily involved with the design, testing and automation/documentation of steps to move from the old infrastructure to the new.

As you review scope, remember to consider changes that are already being required to move an application such as the IP address, host name, ports and required services to run the application.

Budget

Datacenter migrations are expensive. It is easy to spend $25,000,000 in hardware and facilities to build a new datacenter. The estimate for the build out should be gathered through existing processes with infrastructure engineers, datacenter engineers and procurement specialists.

Most of the cost associated with moving the applications and services comes in the form of internal staff since much of the work is best performed by the analysts and engineers who already know the application, its environment and have a working relationship with the business owner and application users. While this application work can be outsourced, it should be estimated at a 5x cost compared to internal resources. It is far more economical to assign existing resources to the datacenter move project and back fill their daily duties to staff augmentation individuals.

As an estimate for internal resource costs, if you are adhering to the ROPE framework, the following represents a solid resource budget for moving applications:

- 1/2 - 1 Program Manager depending on familiarity with the ROPE framework, scope of your project, your organizational staff and processes

- 2 Tower leads[1]
- 1 Workstream Manager[2]
- 1 PM per 10 analysts required for applications
- 1 PM for Infrastructure services
- 1 - 2 Network Engineer equivalent spread over several individuals depending on the number of network services moving and applications' network requirements
- 1.5 – 2 Server Engineer equivalents spread over several individuals (you may need to adjust for the various OS's and their support: Windows, Linux, Unix, AIX, ...)
- 20 – 40 hours of application analyst time for each application
- 100 hours of engineering time per service
- 1 – 2 QA Lead equivalent spread over a couple of individuals

For a more detailed task list associated with each role, refer to the RACI template.

Guiding principles

The guiding principles is by far one of the most powerful tools senior leadership will provide to empower the datacenter migration project team. The principles guide what the project team will do, why it is being done and how. The guiding principles serve as guardrails for making decisions in pursuit of the goal: To move out of the old datacenter.

Make no mistake about it, the project team will use these principles daily so consider them carefully and create guiding principles that will further the project and allow decisions to be made by those closest to the issue while still adhering to the direction set by senior leadership. One key point to successful guiding principles is to ensure senior leadership internalizes them and considers the principles their own.

The actual definition of guiding principles can be difficult to articulate and are best explained through example. The following are some of the most powerful principles we have developed with previous clients' senior leadership.

Aha Moment

The datacenter migration is an application project

This principle makes it clear to everyone the datacenter migration is not an infrastructure project. 10 times out of 10, a datacenter move project is owned by a leader within infrastructure. This principle ensures leaders of the

---

[1] See Staffing for Tower Lead description

[2] See Staffing for Workstream Manager description

application teams and business understand they play a large role in the project. This project will affect analyst staffing, work priority and accountability for applications moving to the new data center. The framework takes advantage of the fact that application analysts understand their applications in detail, know the business workflow and have built a relationship with the user community.

App Teams Got This

App analysts own the migration,
infrastructure teams support them throughout the migration

While similar to the "Aha Moment" this principle focuses on the application analysts and emphasizes the importance of application analysts owning the individual moves. This principle also demonstrates the role infrastructure engineers will have throughout the project. Infrastructure engineers must consider how to make the move as easy as possible on the analysts and assist in every way they can through automation, quick turn arounds and collaboration. The final decision on when and how, lies with the application team who is ultimately responsible.

Like for Like

Keep applications, technology and user experience consistent

"Like for Like" is an extremely important guiding principle to negotiate with senior leadership. Throughout the life of the datacenter migrations, PMs will use the "Like for Like" principle. When confronted by analysts, engineers or business users asking for the okay to make a simple little change (upgrade SQL version or implement the new code update they've been waiting months for) project leaders can simply respond with: "Senior leadership has decided this is a like for like migration. You can make that change before or after the move as a separate project but not as a part of the migration." This avoids lengthy debates about the value of the requested change and addresses the death by 1,000 cuts problem. This is absolutely the most powerful and important guiding principle to negotiate. You can always allow an exception, but that exception will have to be extremely important rather than one of the many cuts that may occur without this principle.

Keep it Repeatable

Use what works until it doesn't then only make small tweaks

This principle is at the heart of the ROPE framework. Each move will be tailored with application specific work, such as the order to bring down servers, moving the VIP if it has one, or configuration change for new IP addresses, but they all follow the same process on relatively the same time line and the basic work flow. Keeping the process repeatable allows the infrastructure teams to get into a groove for support and enables analysts to know what to expect with every application they move. Keeping it repeatable applies to all aspects:

- Communication sent out to users looks the same regardless of the application so that end users know this is a part of the datacenter migration as well as what to expect during the move.
- Change controls have similar information allowing for reuse and allowing change boards to easily recognize the changes associated with the datacenter migration.
- Move events follow the same structure allowing everyone to maintain their role and duty expectations during the move event.

Keeping it repeatable allows the project to build templates and use them over and over, making it easier on everyone. Reuse existing company processes and templates where possible but look to streamline these processes for the project since they will be repeated hundreds of times by the move project.

Involve Me

Stakeholders actively engaged, and awareness is apparent

Once you start executing, poor communication causes more avoidable problems than just about anything else. A datacenter move will touch everyone in the organization. Different stakeholder groups will be touched at different times and some will have different communication needs. Keeping everyone informed appropriately is a significant task but one that needs to be engrained into the project with leadership's backing.

Leadership will own the role of amplifying the messages coming from the project team across their direct reports and peers in the organization.

Decide and Move On

Consider the data, decide and continue, don't dwell on it

Datacenter migration projects are filled with ambiguity. Engineers, analysts and IT people enjoy the mental exercise of evaluating all aspects of the options or issue until they have the data to make the perfect recommendation. You'll recognize this in organizations where the same issue resurfaces again and again, or teams get stuck in analysis paralysis. If this is true for your organization use this principle to keep moving when the team has to make a decision without the complete set of data.

This is not the same as any decision is better than no decision. The decide and move on principle says make the best decision with the data you have available. The advantage of many small moves is that feedback will come early and often, allowing for better decisions each time.

Mind the Risk

Small manageable moves are low risk to our business and customers

Risk management is built into the core of the ROPE framework. Moving a single application (or small few) at a time rather than large move waves reduces the risk associated with datacenter migrations, increases through put and brings value to customers sooner. Frequent, small moves also shorten the feedback loop allowing for quick meaningful improvements. If you allow your customer to choose the move date for their application, within your time frame, you've set the stage for deeper buy in to the schedule and move activities.

Additionally, this principle reinforces the fact that leadership is committed to lowering the risk to the business verses minimizing the cost or schedule.

The guiding principles you negotiate with senior leadership should reflect the principles needed based on your datacenter migration project, senior leaderships' desired outcome and the culture of your organization. For example, in one case where senior leadership required an overly aggressive schedule, we negotiated guiding principles that allowed the project team to take higher risk, press for very aggressive schedules and ensure those involved with the move knew they had the blessing of senior leadership. A few guiding principles we negotiated on that project included:

We're Sorry

Beg forgiveness later rather than receive everyone's permission

This principle prevented the project from being held back by approvers on PTO and allowed us to push for emergency change controls when needed without the repercussions normally associated with a shortened change control cycle.

Accept the Risk

We understand the risk is high to our business and customers

Senior leadership made a clear statement they were willing to accept the risk associated with the accelerated schedule. This did not eliminate the need for planning but allowed for the fact that some details may be missed causing an unplanned outage.

Got Your Back

Mistakes are okay, senior leadership has the team's back on this one

Taking risks is often a double-edged sword. This principle allowed the team to take the steps required to use new processes, technology and tools to shorten the schedule without fear of reprisals. Of course, the underlying message included, mistakes are okay, but don't make the same mistake twice.

By no means are these all the guiding principles we've negotiated over the years, but they do reflect a broad spectrum for you to draw from. Use the examples and add those you feel are needed for your project. When negotiating your guiding principles with senior leadership, focus strategically on the big picture. As a rule, there should only be six to eight guiding principles needed to cover most situations.

A guiding principle is a short pithy statement that conveys larger ideas. The best guiding principles are expressions of senior leadership's internalized ideals for the project. When senior leadership is using the guiding principles to communicate out, you know you have them right.

Engineering Build

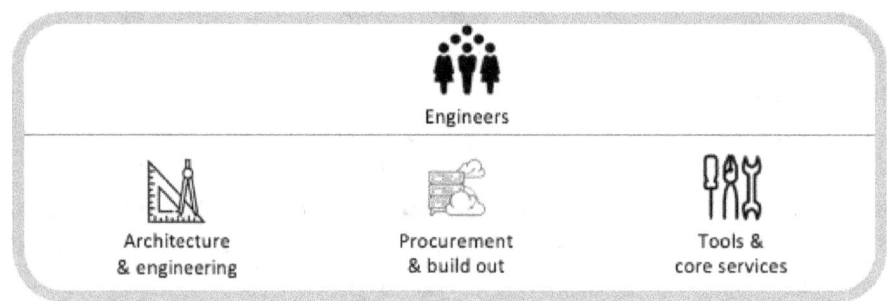

Throughout this guide you will read that a datacenter migration is not an infrastructure project. However, the infrastructure is foundational to the project. Assuming you have decided on the location for the new datacenter the choices made in the infrastructure will determine how simple or difficult it will be to move the applications and services.

Regardless of the choice, plan on assembling a list of reasons each choice was made. As the application teams come into the process and hear about the new datacenter's infrastructure and its impact on their activities they will want to know why. Keeping the application teams informed about the infrastructure design and the reasons behind the design will significantly reduce the amount of noise that accompanies a project of this complexity.

The following are a few of the choices that will be made and points to consider.

Network/Security

The first choice is IP space. Will servers moving from the old to new datacenter require new IP addresses and all the network changes that comes with a new IP address?

Keeping the same IP space in both datacenters by extending layer 2 significantly reduces the time and complexity of the application moves. However, it places the risk square on the shoulders of the network team to manage layer 2, either natively or using a technology such as Cisco OTV. While stretching layer 2 makes many of the migrations easier, it imposes outages across all applications to move network gateways. The commands to move the gateways can be scripted to reduce the outage time but outages must occur at some point during the project when layer 2 is stretched across the datacenters.

If an IP address change is not required for security zoning, IP address clean up or other business/technical reason, maintaining the same IP address for servers and applications is preferred.

Regardless of standards, some applications will use IP addresses instead of fully qualified domain names (FQDN) to communicate with other applications, databases, print servers, file systems or end point modalities. This is more often the case with older applications, but some "modern" applications continue to have IP addresses in configuration files for interface communication. Many end point modalities in health care or robotics use IP addresses to communicate with servers.

Finding all the configuration files containing an embedded IP address can be difficult resulting in an outage when the interface is moved. For example: "A" communicates with "B" using IP address. Move "B" and "B" works fine but "A" starts to fail. If "A's" dataflow is not fully understood, the root cause of "B" moving may be difficult to identify and resolve, especially in the case of occasional communications such as weekly, monthly or quarterly reports.

Network architecture changes present a difficult choice. For most clients, a network architecture upgrade is called for since this is often the only time it can be easily accomplished.

In order to successfully accomplish a network architecture change and minimize the impact on the application moves we recommend the following:

- Network staff be fully trained on the new architecture.
- New architecture and design be fully vetted out by the manufacturer.
- Highly skilled professional services be employed to assist with the design and implementation of the new network architecture.
- Avoid changing both the security model and network architecture. Reserve the security model changes for post datacenter migration.
- Discuss the proposed network architecture with the application teams explaining the design, implications to their applications and user access, as well as the reasons for the architecture and design choices.
- For application impacts or changes needed during the migration, determine the steps required for an application to migrate from the old datacenter into the new datacenter's network. These steps should be well documented, automated if possible and presented to all application teams prior to the beginning of the migration phase, preferably as soon as they are known and fully understood.

Compute

Naming conventions for hosts often include location. Maintaining hostnames for servers that migrate from the old datacenter to the new is the least impactful on the application teams. In a modern environment, users and applications communicate with hosts using the fully qualified domain name (FQDN) which typically includes the hostname.

If hostnames are going to change, application configuration files containing interface locations will need to be changed or aliases created in Domain Name Services (DNS). Locating all the configuration files containing FQDNs can be difficult resulting in an outage when the interface is moved. For example: "A" communicates with "B" using an FQDN with the hostname in it. Move "B" and "B" works fine but "A" starts to fail. If "A's" dataflow is not fully understood, the root cause of "B" moving may be difficult to identify and resolve, especially in the case of occasional communications such as weekly, monthly, or quarterly reports. Adding an alias record to DNS with the old FQDN pointing to the new server location can reduce this issue.

Changes to the virtual compute platform is most often transparent to users. Choice of hypervisor, physical platform and convergence technology typically does not impact the virtual guests. In order to successfully accomplish a compute architecture change and minimize the impact on the application moves we recommend the following:

- Server engineers be fully trained on the new platform / architecture.
- New architecture and design be fully vetted out by the manufacturer.
- Highly skilled professional services be employed to assist with the design and implementation of the new compute architecture and its supporting services.
- Discuss the proposed platform / architecture with the application teams explaining the design, implications to their applications and user access, as well as the reasons for the architecture and design choices.
- For application impacts or changes needed during the application migration determine the steps required for an application to migrate from the old datacenter into the new datacenter's architecture. These steps should be well documented, automated if possible and presented to all application teams prior to the beginning of the migration.
- Validate the new platform runs all, including non-standard, variations of guests existing in the old datacenter. Plan how non-conforming guests will be supported with minimal impact to the application teams.
- Ensure provisioning, monitoring, file access, SAN, backups, replication, networking and security have been considered during the design phase and tested thoroughly post implementation.
- Plan for changes to operational processes, alerting, and automation.
- Work to migrate as many physical servers to virtual guests as possible. The tools and techniques available to migrate physical to virtual have improved immensely and every effort should be made to reduce the physical footprint. In some cases, this will mean purchasing an appliance to support dongle license keys. Other cases will require

eliminating the need for line-cards and POTs (plain old telephone) lines by working with the telecom engineers.

For physical server moves, plan a bare metal backup and restore in case the hardware is damaged in transit or fails to come back up in the new datacenter. A bare metal backup is intended to mitigate a worst-case scenario. The bare metal backup may not match its application's, recovery point objective (RPO) or recovery time objective (RTO), rather it is intended to rebuild the server to a known good state at which point backup data can be applied in order to bring the server up to its RPO. A pre-move reboot of physical servers is advised along with a plan if the server fails to come back up during a pre-move reboot.

When moving physical blades, validate configurations prior to moves to ensure compatibility between blades and the receiving chassis.

The compute team needs to develop a plan that supports non-standard physical servers running in the current datacenter. This may be to virtualize or provide additional resources to assist the analyst to upgrade to a new server before the move or isolate the server in the new facility until it can be upgraded after the move. What the plan cannot be is to simply tell the application team it is their problem and they cannot move it into the new datacenter.

Most server teams will express a desire is to bring the virtual guests up to standard for operating system, patch levels, or image during the move. We strongly discourage changes to individual guests during the move. Changes to guests should be implemented several weeks before or after the application has moved. This also holds true for applications running on physical servers. A separate environment and/or security container can be set up to receive non-standard servers as long as no new or additional changes are imposed on the applications.

The server engineers will be heavily involved in executing the application move from one datacenter to the other. A number of tools will support moving virtual workloads. The following requirements should be used in selection of a tool(s) for moving virtual workloads:

If IP address and/or host name is changing or an outage is acceptable/required to move workloads:

- Workload migration cutovers must be schedulable.
- Tool will migrate the workload and its data.
- Initial workload and data copies can be started prior to the actual move event. Once the initial copy is completed the tool maintains the two file sets (guests) in synch through the use of delta copy and commit.
- Synchronization frequency can be increased in order to reduce the time required to commit the delta changes.

- Multiple workloads can be in different stages of the process at any time. For example: some may be in the initial copy stage, others synchronizing and still others being cut over.
- Easily restore workloads and data back to old datacenter during cutover event. Post cutover workloads and data can be restored in the old datacenter with known (preferably no loss) data or the move process can be reversed in order to migrate workloads and data back to the old datacenter.

If IP address and/or host name is not changing and no outage is required to move workloads:

- Workload and data migrations are seamless to the application and users.
- Workload and data can be migrated while the application remains live in production.
- Specific workloads and data can be selected to move.
- Easily restore workloads and data back to old datacenter.

Migrations of an active workload and data typically requires networking to stretch layer 2 between the old and new datacenter allowing vCenter (or other virtualization system) to communicate seamlessly across all virtual platforms involved in the migration. For VMware, vMotion has been successfully used to "live migrate" workloads and data between datacenters. New technologies continue to make migration of live workloads easier by abstracting the underling names and addresses. Regardless of tool, look at it from the perspective of the analyst and the end user asking yourself, how will this reduce their work.

Independent of the tool(s) chosen, the process of migrating workloads and data should be fully documented with as much automation as possible. Migrations will be occurring throughout the week and over the weekends, several server engineers will be required to cover the cutover times and the process needs to be predictable regardless of which engineer executes it.

Storage

Most organizations update their storage platforms during a datacenter build out. We have not found challenges with storage platform changes as long as the architecture and design fully accounts for changes to data copy, replication and backups. This design also includes the movement of data and backups with workloads as well as provisioning within the virtual and physical compute environment.

The most troublesome area of new storage platforms results from incorrect or incomplete fiber connections to and from the SAN switches. Another trouble spot occurs during physical server moves with HBAs and the fibers having been rolled into the wrong ports or worldwide names are missed.

Similar to extending the data network's layer 2, the SAN fabric can also be extended over dark fiber with DWDM gear or through the use of other technology allowing a physical server to move and access its SAN data regardless of location. The extension of the SAN fabric can allow for a seamless migration of SAN data and the storage team may want to investigate their options.

Physical Space

In any new datacenter build there will be a temptation to standardize, secure and monitor everything. This is especially true when shifting from an in-house datacenter to a lights-out co-location facility.

We recommend carefully considering what is truly value add and what will become needless noise and consume bandwidth. For example: Cameras are valuable for the operations staff to quickly get a sense of the co-location space. Some may want a detailed view of everything. However, with hot aisle containment (HAC), having a crystal-clear view of all points in the datacenter requires a significant number of cameras capable of low light imaging that can quickly drive up cost without providing additional value. Having a few cameras that give a general sense of the space and a view of who enters and exits may be a good compromise solution. Badge access on each cabinet can feel like a good security control until there is an outage requiring access to various cabinets not normally accessible to remote hands staff. Consider using badge swipes to simply audit who has been into a cabinet. Monitoring every cabinet for temperature and humidity will not provide additional benefit over monitoring every third cabinet. Consider alarming off individual server temperature readings and monitoring cabinets for overall space conditions.

In a lights-out datacenter, work with the co-location facilities manager to understand the site's security, monitoring, reporting and access processes, then augment appropriately. Other facility customers have PCI or regulatory requirements which have been solved making the facilities manager a valuable resource. The most important policy to put in place, is limiting the number of internal staff who have access into the space.

One area that may be worth investing in is remotely managed cabinet PDUs. PDUs that allow operational staff to read power utilization and control power on a single port can facilitate remotely power cycling a device when a device is hung. There is a cost in auditing and maintaining the correct information on each port to ensure accurate mapping of ports to the devices.

Cable identification is a must. But keep it simple. Cable colors should be standard and used religiously. A separate color for the data network, management network, and cross over cables is a good standard. Order cables of various colors and lengths with serialized numbers at each end. Cable management should keep the power, low voltage and fiber neatly tucked away allowing airflow and equipment access. The goal is for operations to be able to work with smart hands over the phone, so they know the proper color cable to pull at the device and can check the serial number before pulling the other end to move devices in or out without disturbing other equipment.

Datacenters are living organisms that change over time. The physical space should be managed to a level that will allow operations to keep track of changes without change management becoming a fulltime task. Look for tools that can scan, catalog and maintain accurate information. Build a single source of truth that all information is maintained in. Avoid each group having their own source of record that does not automatically roll up into your CMDB (configuration management database).

Open for business

The best laid plans don't always come together. Equipment shortages, staff turnover, emergency business changes and keeping the lights on in the old datacenter may slow down the new datacenter build.

Develop a list of the minimum services required to open the datacenter to applications and those that may have to come later. For example: Connectivity between the new and old datacenter is required day one but if the internet circuits are delayed, the network team can route in/out bound Internet traffic through the old datacenter. Domain controllers are required but users can be provisioned using the identity management services in the old datacenter.

The ability to use (backhaul) services from the old datacenter in support of the new datacenter will permit the infrastructure teams to be more thoughtful in their deployment without holding back application migrations.

Having a list of bare minimum required services focuses teams' efforts. While this may mean the datacenter is not open to all application migrations, it will provide the core infrastructure to receive pilot moves that will further test the infrastructure, migration processes, communication and over all assumptions of the project.

Tool build out

Infrastructure tool selection for the migration can be as simple or as complicated as the teams make it. In this discussion, we will cover some of the top issues we see occur during the tool selection and migration process.

Infrastructure focuses not customer focused

Migration tools are intended to make moving applications and services easier on the customer and the application analyst, not just the infrastructure engineers.

Some tools will make infrastructure tasks very simple but place a higher burden on the rest of the teams. As a service organization, make sure the tools you select for the move provide a more seamless experience for your customer.

Too many bells and whistles not enough meat and potatoes

Many tools can support the movement of virtual servers from one location to another. Some do only that and do it very well. Other tools can move virtual servers as well as provide backup facilities, data replication, virtualization upgrades, and so on. The desire to purchase a tool that will meet long-term goals can get in the way of selecting the tool needed to move applications today.

To avoid selecting the wrong tool be very clear about what are the specific tool requirements for the move. If the tool will support long-term goals as well that is great but don't skimp on the real requirements or over complicate the process of using the tool because of add on features.

Some basic questions to ask before selecting a tool:

- How will this reduce the work of application analysts and customers?
- How will this reduce the work of infrastructure teams without increasing the work from analysts and customers (If you think something will be an insignificant impact to the analyst or customer you should ask them. Most likely it is not.)?
- How can this tool automate the work and make the process repeatable?
- What benefit are the additional functions of the tool to this datacenter migration?
- How does the tool allow for scheduling of its activities to ensure precise timing?
- How can activities back out / fail back using the tool and how long will it require?

Areas to consider using tools include:

- Converting firewall rules from one platform to another and propagating/managing those rules across both datacenters.
- End to end network monitoring of bandwidth, traffic reporting, latency indicators, port reporting, packet captures, full route tracing (beyond trace route and ping).
- Migrating virtual workloads from one datacenter to another.
- Migrating workloads from physical to virtual servers.
- Migrating physical workloads from one physical server to another physical server.
- Bare-metal backups.
- Mass data transfers and data synchronization.
- Testing of infrastructure
  - Synthetic logins.

- o Traffic generation.
- o Scanning of servers.

As discussed in the compute section above, Veeam is a tool that we have used in several datacenter migration projects to successfully move virtual workloads. Veeam meets the requirements for moving virtual workloads:

- Can be scheduled.
- Can be automated.
- The majority of the work can be completed prior to the move event.
- Extremely easy to fall back.

OTV is another tool we have successfully used to stretch network layer 2 across datacenters when they are technically connected over layer 3. OTV allows workloads to maintain their same IP address reducing the amount of changes and testing required. However, it is a complicated setup, introduces a large amount of overhead on the network team and must be tweaked throughout the project. In order to use OTV successfully you must have a very good knowledge of all aspects of your existing datacenter's network to ensure you don't introduce problems.

Scan tools are often brought up as a way to map applications and identify interface connections. These types of tools are most productive when they already exist in the environment and are currently providing the mapping information. If new scan tools are going to be used to map applications, plan the effort to work through all the barriers such as: firewall rules, credentials, access to appliances, vendor owned equipment, and general environmental change concerns. It can take several months before meaningful results are produced and manual validations will be required.

Many scan tools highlight their value by showing off connectivity graphing capability. These drawings are much less valuable in a datacenter move than the ability to export and pivot data. Data that can be put into spreadsheets and analyzed in multiple ways provides deeper insights than a graphical interface.

PlateSpin can be used for a number of activities including bare-metal backups, migrations and converting physical to virtual platforms. PlateSpin is powerful but may require a steep learning curve if your team is not familiar with it.

Tools are extremely helpful but there is no magic bullet. The teams are still required to put in the work to understand the applications, build test plans, communicate with users and execute the move event.

Discovery and Planning

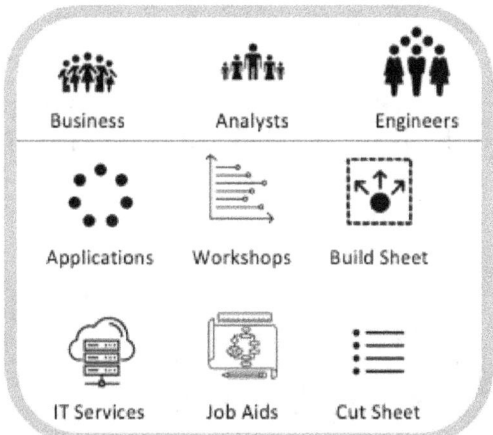

In this section, you will find an overview of discovery and planning, laying out key ideas. The training guides provide additional details on the activities and tasks to complete.

Discovery and planning are where the work begins to migrate applications and services. If your organization has an accurate CMDB (configuration management database) it should be the starting point for discovery. The goal of the discovery and planning activities is to continually validate scope, document each application's As-Is state in the current datacenter and establish the tasks to move the application to the new datacenter. In order to accomplish these goals, the ROPE framework uses a couple of powerful tools: the build sheet and the cut sheet.

The build sheet documents requirements of the current As-Is state for each individual application. The build sheet records information such as the host name and IP address of the server(s) the application is running on, load balancing VIPs used by the application and the other applications or services the application interfaces with.

The cut sheet is the how an application will be moved. The cut sheet is a task list containing pre-move, move and post-move tasks along with who is responsible for completing the task by when. Example of cut sheet tasks include:

- Pre-move tasks:
    - Submitting change control for the move.
    - Sending out user communications.
    - Executing baseline tests.
    - Initiate data copy.
    - Validate network port settings.
    - Arranging for vendor participation.

- o Gaining go/no go agreement from all stakeholders.
- Move tasks:
  - o Shutting down databases and applications.
  - o Executing the final server and data synchronization.
  - o Changing server IP address and host name.
  - o Swinging DNS to the new server addresses.
  - o Modifying application configurations with new IP addresses or FQDNs.
  - o Application interface testing.
- Post-move tasks
  - o Closing the change control.
  - o Update monitoring.
  - o Updating the CMDB.
  - o Updating system documentation.
  - o Archiving test results.
  - o Follow up with application users.

Both the build sheets and the cut sheets are created and maintained in Smartsheet[3]. While we recommend the use of Smartsheet, you may use Microsoft Excel in combination with SharePoint (or Wiki), but you will lose some key functionality provided by Smartsheet. The lost functionality includes:

- Automated real time reporting dashboard.
- Simultaneous editing of sheets.
- Unlimited collaboration with internal and external resources.
- Centralized repository of application/project artifacts.
- Automatic change history recording.

The development of the build sheets and the cut sheets is a collaboration between engineers, analysts and end customers. While the application analyst is expected to own the sheets and drive their development, they will need to reach out and collaborate with others in order to completely develop the cut over task list and ensure each task is assigned to the right person.

Another sheet used to record the To-Be changes is referred to as the tech info sheet. This sheet is used to record the servers' new IP address, host names or other technical information changing on an application basis. The tech info sheet has a less rigid structure and develops from the needs of the infrastructure teams to communicate the new To-Be information.

---

[3] Smartsheet is a third-party project management tool for non-project managers. It is only available in SAAS from. For more information about Smartsheet review their website smartsheet.com

When using Smartsheet the best practice is to create a folder for each application. Each application folder will have a build sheet, cut sheet, tech info and any other unique sheets associated with that specific application. In this way everything known about the application is quickly available in one on-line location.

If using Excel spreadsheets, the build sheet, cut sheet and tech info should be kept on separate tabs in one workbook.

Often the hardest step in the discovery and planning phase is selecting a date to move an application. It is also one of the easiest steps.

The ROPE framework is built around the premise that small amounts of work can be deployed into production incrementally. In the case of a datacenter move, a single application can move independently of all other applications without affecting its performance or integrity. Rather than a few large move groups, there is a continuous migration of applications, one application at a time. Small applications move in and among larger more complex applications.

Micro Moves
Minimize customer impacts, reduce complexity & increase rate of success.

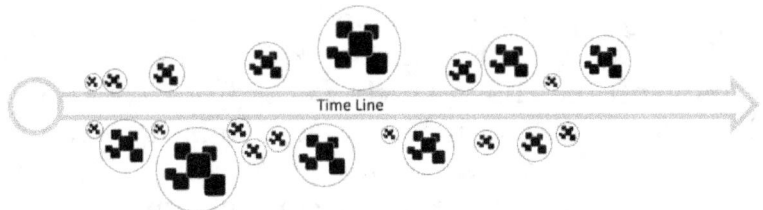

Rather than a few large move groups, there is a continuous migration of applications, one application at a time. Small applications move in and among larger more complex applications.

The goal of the micro moves is to minimize the impact of each individual move to only those customers who use the application being moved. In most cases this will be a small manageable number of individuals. Application analysts should negotiate with their customers to determine the best date and time, taking into account any blackout dates, heavy workload periods or other mandated restrictions. Target dates will be accumulated in the move matrix and be firmed up as the build sheets and cut sheets are complete.

We have moved datacenters across town and across the country. In every case the ROPE framework's incremental approach has provided a significant advantage over large move waves. As the distance between the datacenters grows, latency becomes a factor to consider. Databases may need to move with the application or latency sensitive applications may need to be bundled. If there is a concern about latency between the datacenters, the best approach is to perform tests with lower environments (Dev, Test, Integration, ...) or low risk pilot applications and validate your working assumptions.

Job aids

A datacenter migration project will touch everyone in the organization at one point or another. Many of the groups that will be affected have processes unique to them and are not entirely understood by others. In other cases, similar outcomes may be governed by different processes depending on the group. Even a common, thoroughly documented process may not be known by all who will be involved in the datacenter migration. For these reasons, it is important to establish the processes that will be followed and create a common method for executing on each of them.

The following are common processes we gain agreement on and then document the steps needed to complete. If anyone on the project is unsure, the job aid will guide them through the process.

- Technical change control: It is important to establish who will submit the change control for the move. If other changes are required along the way, are they piggy backed on the move change or is a separate change entered and by who? Does the analyst know how to submit change controls? Talk with the change review board so they know what to expect with every datacenter move. Have a common heading. Gain agreement to attach the cut sheet and build sheet to the change in order to avoid having to retype all the steps, contacts, affected systems and fall back plan (these are all in the cut sheet).
- Determine the teams that require a ticket to do work for the project and those who will assign a project resource. Build a job aid for entering a ticket for each team using a common heading, description and approval. Negotiate with the teams a shorter SLA based on the datacenter move project's priority. Typically firewall rules as well as identity management activities default to needing a ticket.
- Sending out communication for the datacenter migration should follow the same look every time and come from the same email address. Document the work flow so that analyst, engineers and others know where to grab the templates and know how to send the messages from a consistent address.
- Decommissioning equipment workflow: Many physical devices will be left behind once the service or application running on them has been migrated. Document the work flow a service owner or application analyst

should follow to have the physical device decommissioned, recycled or repurposed.

While not a process, one of the most powerful workflow documents is the choice for move methods[4]. Going into the project many groups will have their own ideas about how they will move their applications. Going back to one of the guiding principles "Keep It Repeatable", you want to layout the acceptable choices for moving an application and the work flow it will follow. Typically, we recommend documenting three or four workflows:

- Virtual migration (referred to as V2V)
- Physical migration (referred to as forklift or lift and shift)
- Physical to virtual migration (referred to as P2V)
- Build new

The document should layout at a high-level the workflow, outage requirements, risks and planning needs. By documenting the workflow for each method, you allow analysts and customers to choose the most appropriate method while maintaining consistency and control.

Templates

Along with this guide you will find example templates we have used successfully for several datacenter move projects. Based on your organization's needs, develop templates that will facilitate a common look and feel across your datacenter move project. By using templates, you accomplish two goals:

- Everyone will quickly recognize the request/communication/document/... is associated with the datacenter move and can prioritize it appropriately.
- Reduces the workload of those creating requests/communications/documents/... Since often there are several hundred applications and services moving, the savings in effort can be substantial over time.

While not an exhaustive list, the following are templates we recommend for your datacenter move project:

- Customer/user focused notification:
    o Notification of upcoming move events (sent by application analysts, should go out three times leading up to the move event).
    o Start of move events (sent by application analysts).
    o Completion of move events (sent by application analysts).

---

[4] See example of Move Methods for more information.

- Internal IT focused notification (often more technical than customer focused communication):
  - Notification of upcoming move events (sent to IT managers).
  - Start of move events (sent by engineers to their peers).
  - Completion of move events (sent by engineers to their peers).
- Change control.
- Datacenter move project feedback.

As you can see, the majority of the templates focus on communication. After successfully completing numerous datacenter migrations, it is evident that clear, consistent, transparent communication with all stakeholders is one of the most important activities to perform well on a datacenter migration project.

Move Train

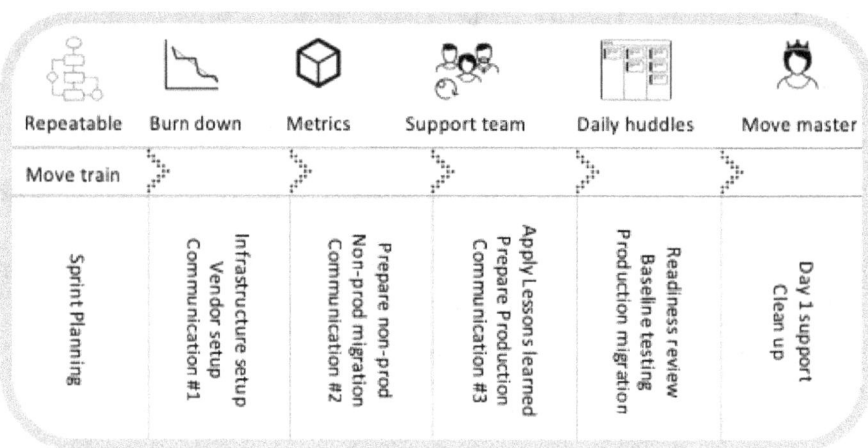

The move train activity is where the rubber meets the road and all the planning pays off. In general, for a datacenter migration project, the move train is made up of four, one-week sprints. This allows ample time for multiple communications to go out, change controls to be submitted and approved, vendors to engage with the teams and finalize their move tasks as well as allow everyone to complete all the pre-move tasks on the cut sheet. If there are lower environments such as dev/test or QA, they are moved in the second and third sprints as a dress rehearsal with lessons learned applied to the production move cut sheet. Each environment will have its own cut sheet which can be copied forward and adjusted.

The majority of applications will follow this time line. Each week new applications will enter the move train as other applications continue on or exit the process. Significantly complex applications, such as moving a mainframe, may require more than four weeks to complete their pre-move tasks and prepare for the move event, however it is still completing the same general task list, but with more details drawn in to account for the added complexity.

As an application enters the move train, it starts out with sprint planning. In sprint planning the application analyst informs all the project participants about the application, what it is used for, the infrastructure it relies on, and how it is planned to move. Sprint planning allows the supporting engineers to learn about the application and gather information about the application they may need in order to prepare for the move. This is also an opportunity for engineers to clarify components or interface information that may be required.

Unlike some approaches that look to document all information across all applications that can possibly be known before any start to move, the ROPE framework documents the common information and looks to engage people in conversations to add specific information valuable to a specific application as close to the time frame required as possible. We have found that by injecting collaboration rather than documentation into the process, less mistakes based on assumptions and stale data are committed and the overall workload across the teams goes down.

However, this means many groups will be collaborating with each other for the first time which may be a little awkward at first. PMs are expected to coach analysts and engineers through the awkwardness and facilitate discussions across groups when and where they are required. As the project progresses through multiple iterations, collaboration will become more natural and require less coaching.

Once the sprint planning session is complete, usually held on Mondays for all applications entering the move train that week, the analysts will join the daily huddle. The daily huddle is a 15-minute standup meeting/call where all analysts for all applications in the move train report out. The huddle is not a status report. It is the opportunity to ask for help and quickly get connected with the person who can help, so that the issue can be resolved off line. In this way, the project avoids a problem spinning in email for days before it is escalated.

Throughout the move train, PMs are ushering each of the applications through the process, reviewing cut sheets with the teams, checking off completed tasks, ensuring communication is flowing and escalating issues to have them quickly resolved by the responsible teams in order to gain a final "go" from everyone involved in that application's move event.

Following a successful move that has been validated against its baseline tests and signed off by the application analysts, engineers, and customer, the application is turned over to operations support. If an issue is encountered post sign-off, it is handled by the existing operational process, allowing the project engineers and analysts to continue forward with the remaining application moves.

The first applications to go through the move train should be treated as pilot moves. Ten to 20 low risk applications selected by the application analysts and business owners should test out your move train process. Because you will be moving individual applications quickly through the move train, lessons learned will come quickly in the pilot phase. The learning from each of these application moves should be codified and put back into the move train, job aids, cut sheet and processes.

The pilot moves should validate working assumptions and demonstrate the ability to move applications independently. The following is a simple pilot matrix that shows the various items selected for this client to test out the move train process and validate assumptions.

Application Name	Service Line	Windows P to V	Windows V to V	Windows Build New	Forklift Physical	DB without Application	Application without Database	Application without File share	Unix P to V	Unix V to V	SFTP	Shared Server	Access Method - Citrix	Access Method APPV	Access Method VPN	Access Method Corepoint	Access Regulated from Corporate Zone
AeroScout MobileView	General Apps			X										X			
Orchard Harvest			X													X	X
Globalscape SFTP			X								X						
Bonestation	Radiology Apps		X										X	X		X	X
Olah Viewer	General Apps						X		X						X		X

38

Application Name	Service Line	Windows P to V	Windows V to V	Windows Build New	Forklift Physical	DB without Application	Application without Database	Application without File share	Unix P to V	Unix V to V	SFTP	Shared Server	Access Method - Citrix	Access Method APPV	Access Method VPN	Access Method Corepoint	Access Regulated from Corporate Zone
Apollo Advance	Cardiology Apps		X				X	X								X	
Cnext Cancer Registry	Oncology Apps			X													X
Spss Modeler	General Apps		X				X	X									
Sleep Center Server WA1SMASQL03	General Apps		X			X											
Sleep Center Server (DEVSMAW-VG01)	Specialty Med Apps		X														
Media Site	General Apps		X				X					X					
PeopleSoft Supply Chain (DB-only)	Supply Chain				X	X											

Application Name	Service Line	Windows P to V	Windows V to V	Windows Build New	Forklift Physical	DB without Application	Application without Database	Application without File share	Unix P to V	Unix V to V	SFTP	Shared Server	Access Method - Citrix	Access Method APPV	Access Method VPN	Access Method Corepoint	Access Regulated from Corporate Zone
eNICQ	General Apps	X				X											
PERSYST	General Apps	X															
STIVIEWER	General Apps								X								

Consider this pilot matrix a base. Review the assumptions you have made about how applications will move and operate in the new datacenter then add criteria to the matrix to prove out those assumptions and select low risk applications to participate in the pilot. While you will set the criteria, the application analysts and customers should provide the low risk applications that can be used in the pilot.

Staffing

The program organization of a datacenter migration is extremely important. Your datacenter migration will touch everyone across the organization making it critical to have the proper levels of management engaged.

There are three levels of leadership required. Those leadership levels are:

- Strategic – (Program Leadership) accountable for the program's success
- Tactical – (Workstream Leadership) accountable for the various workstream's success
- Execution – responsible for accomplishing the day to day activities required to move the program forward.

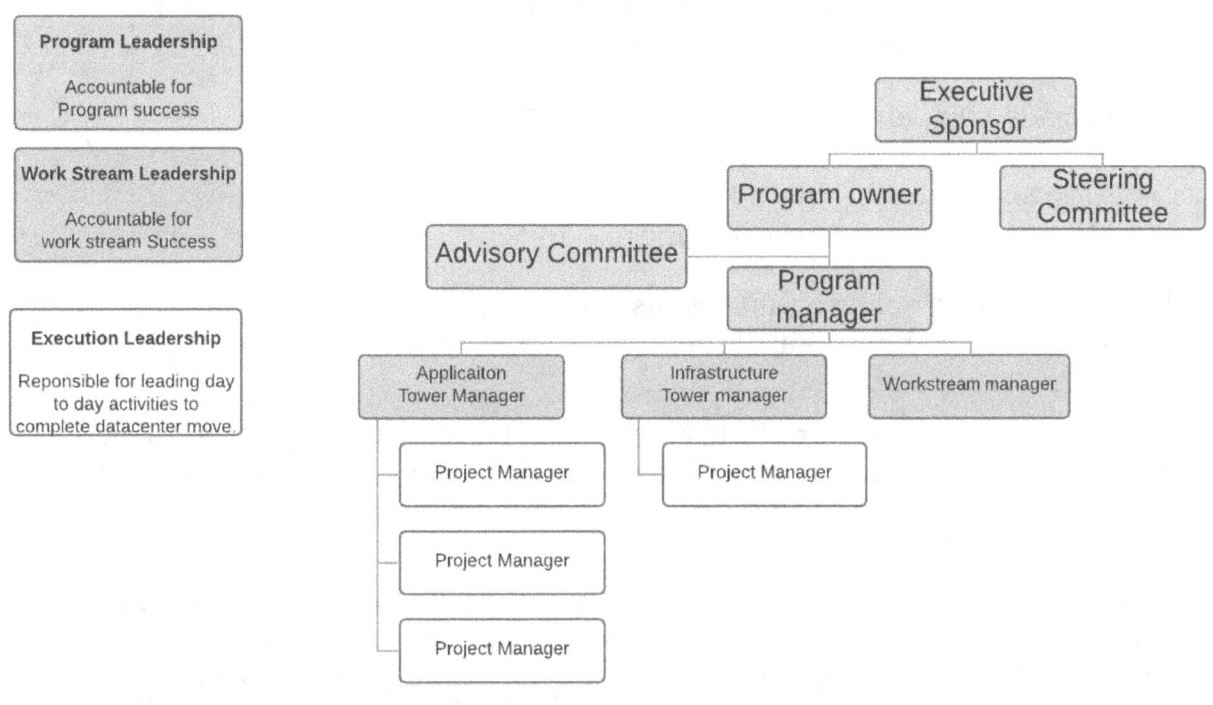

Program Leadership – Strategic level

Executive Sponsor

As with most complex programs of this size, the program's executive sponsor is ideally the CIO or CTO. The executive sponsor must be senior enough to have command and influence across the entire organization for both budget and business priorities. The role of executive sponsor should align with the organization's PMO (project management office) definition. If the guiding principles, scope and budget have been developed correctly, executive sponsorship is minimally required for escalation and the executive sponsor's main contribution is providing message amplification rather than problem solving or course correction.

As an example of amplifying the message, the following text is presented. A datacenter migration was underway, and many staff members were feeling the pressure of the additional workload placed on them by this effort. The project sponsor, a VP in the organization, sent out this communication to all IS/IT staff and amplified the message work stream leaders had been delivering to managers concerning their staff and the process.

There is a Chinese curse which says, "May he live in interesting times." Like it or not, we live in interesting times. These are times of swift change and uncertainty; but this is also the most creative time in our organization's history.

When the Senior Leadership team sat down to discuss the datacenter migration, we decided to do things differently:

- Engage apps and IT teams to solve the problem together
- Get creative and use less capital
- Rely on less traditional PM support
- Minimize the risk to our business partners

We knew we could achieve these goals and complete the datacenter migration because we believed our skilled managers, supervisors and technical staff would step up and excel.

To date we have moved hundreds of virtual servers, proving our gamble on OTV was a winner. The production Exchange environment is well on its way to migrating out of the old datacenter and our application partners in this project, are queuing up more to move.

But now is not the time rest on our accomplishments. As a team we still have applications, services, circuits, and technology to move. Traditionally we would have asked PMs to develop detailed schedules showing interdependencies, critical path and schedule meetings with stakeholders to come up with a fully integrated plan that leaves no stone un-analyzed. But these are interesting times.

As we reach another milestone mark in the project, <<CEO name>>, <<CIO name>> and I invite you to lean-in further to the challenge. You know what's left and where the obstacles are, better than anyone. Bring them forward to the PMs, your manager or me, but bring them with a solution to how you will get them into the move train. Lean-in further by determining how you can solve the problem with what you know rather than highlighting what you don't have.

Our PMs on this project have been asked to approach this challenge differently too. Their primary focus is to get items into the move queues, keep work flowing, remove road blocks, escalate concerns and connect people who can help solve problems. We need you to figure out how and when we're going to move our services and technologies then schedule them into the move queues with the PMs.

By designing the datacenter migration project this way, it is moving faster than ever before and yes it has its share of uncertainty, but I believe our people have and will continue to step up to the challenge of these interesting times.

Sincerely,

VP of Operations

Following this communication from the sponsor, teams were digging in and working together again. Instead of responding with shouldn't someone figure out X, Y or Zed, they asked how they could get their application or service onto the move train sooner and what they needed to do next to prepare their application to move ahead of plan. The PM's could take it from there.

Program Owner

A program owner that reports directly to the executive sponsor is ideal since they will have an existing relationship which is key. The program owner brings in the ability to influence their peers across the organization as well as navigate complex business politics and maintain priorities. The program owner typically comes from the infrastructure side of IT but drives the application migrations through her peers on the application and business side of the house.

Steering Board

The steering board is usually made up of the program owner's peers covering the applications and business. The steering board is charged with removing roadblocks, maintaining scope and resolving program conflicts across the organization. This group should be limited to four or five senior leaders, the executive sponsor being one of the members. The most significant contributions to the program made by the steering board are the guiding principles and ensuring adherence to the ROPE framework as well as funding the budget. In most successful datacenter migration projects, the steering board has performed as the project's advocate across organization and amplified messages to stakeholders in order to reinforce the activities laid out in the ROPE framework.

Advisory Board

The advisory board is comprised of leaders from the affected groups. Typically, members of the advisory board work within the steering board members' team but may also include additional areas not represented in the steering board. The advisory board is chartered with removing roadblocks, maintaining scope and resolving program conflicts across the organization. The advisory board should be able to resolve most issues presented. Only those issues which cannot be solved by the advisory board are presented to the steering board for resolution. If the steering board is receiving significant requests for issue resolution, the advisory board is not performing their role.

When issues or concerns arise, the advisory board should ask "how can we, or our teams, fix this" as opposed to directing the project to do "X", "Y" or "Zed". The advisory board is part of the project team, not outside of it.

Amplifying the project's message across their organizations is another responsibility of the advisory board.

Program Manager

The program manager is primarily focused strategically, bridging across the tactical and strategic leadership roles to ensure direction is set and followed throughout the program. This role needs to understand the ROPE framework and its execution in order to guide the strategic direction and assist with course corrections that align the organization to the framework. Any customizations to the framework must be approved by the program manager and agreed to by the steering board and tower leads. Changes to the ROPE framework should have an eye toward increasing throughput, reducing work in progress and improving the experience of the business.

Work Stream Leadership

The leaders in the work stream leadership layer are accountable for ensuring the work required in their domain is being executed appropriately. In a datacenter move the work is divided into two work streams: Infrastructure and application.

The infrastructure work stream encompasses the build out of the new datacenter followed by migration of the services delivered by the various infrastructure teams. The infrastructure work stream activities also ensure the infrastructure engineers are aligned to support the application migrations.

As the name implies, the application work stream is accountable for ensuring all the applications, in support of the business, are accounted for and migrated. The application work stream activities are designed to ensure the applications are ready to join the move train and aligned with the business.

Data Center Tower Lead(s) Activities

A tower lead focuses on all activities within their tower either applications or infrastructure ensuring the teams in their tower have the tools, training and guidance to complete migration tasks. A tower lead provides a point of escalation, risk management, scope management and oversight as well as consolidated reporting and communication for their tower. While their focus is tower based, tower leads work together to present a consolidated voice and message to stakeholders across the program.

Tower leads possess the following skills and experience required to lead either the application or infrastructure tower:

- Experience moving multiple datacenters using the build sheet, cut sheet, move matrix tools in an agile framework.
- Excellent communication skills in working with all stakeholders from technical SMEs to senior leadership.
- Experience developing tools, job aids and processes to support and optimize move efforts of technical SMEs.
- Experience in communicating and gaining buy-in from stakeholders on the ownership of using the build sheet and cut sheet tools as well as all supporting activities.
- Experience training technical SMEs in the use of build sheets and cut sheets.
- Experience training technical SMEs in the use of Smartsheet as a data center move tool.
- Technical background and experience to allow tower lead to guide SME in the resolution of technical road blocks.
- Experience working with move teams to maintain command and control during a move as well as direct the resolution of technical issues that may arise.
- Experience developing repeatable processes and optimizing repetitive data center move project activities.

Activities performed (or through direction of team members) by a tower lead includes:

- Coach project leaders to resolve issues within their tower and provide a point of escalation.
- Establish move types.
- Establish repeatable work cycles for each move type.
- Document, based on move type, sprint planning process.
- Identify boundaries for applications and systems to be relocated.
- Create and establish move cycles and waves.
- Maintain master build sheet data.
- Establish test plan template.
- Establish cut sheet template.
- Establish defect log template.
- Establish or create data center relocation specific service requests, change requests.
- Establish security requirements and process by move type.
- Establish network requirements and process by move type.
- Contact customers to identify/negotiate move dates and waves (work with application analyst and PMs to accomplish).
- Identify and document, based on move type, server team move tasks.

- Identify and document, based on move type, DBA move tasks.
- Identify and document, based on move type, interface (ex. HL7) move tasks (if applicable).
- Provide training on build sheet and cut sheet framework to stakeholders, PMs and technical SMEs.
- Work with technical SMEs and PMs to create build sheets.
- Work with technical SMEs and PMs to create cut sheets (putting together their knowledge of their application or technology, what they have learned from contacting vendors and the standard tasks identified from the other teams involved in the move).
- Check in with application analysts and PMs to maintain sprint momentum.
- Schedule and manage cut sheet reviews.
- Develop, communicate and maintain move matrix.
- Identify decommissioning/retirement process.
- Identify, document, manage and mitigate issues and risks.
- Tower status.
- Project schedule.
- Identify and create reporting methods.
- Create and maintain the move matrix.
- Manage budget.
- Manage the flow of information where needed.
- Ensure move conference calls are scheduled.
- Ensure change tickets have been submitted and approved.
- Ensure test plans have been created and executed ("go" status will be based on stakeholder feedback).
- Running scrum huddles.
- Running move calls.
- RFPs (if applicable).
- Manage vendors.
- Manage scope and changes.
- Identify and manage risk.
- Identify handshakes and check in with DR, change controls, QA, ITSM, Procurements.
- Identify acceptance criteria.
- Stakeholder analysis.
- Identify overall communication approach and scope.
- Develop communication plan based on stakeholder analysis.
- Develop communication templates.
- Communication coordination and process (ex. Flyers, newsletters, emails, meetings).
- Collect and maintain resource estimates.
- Identify how each type of resource will be engaged on the project (i.e. service requests, set hours) and how time will be recorded.

Workstream manager

The project workstream manager position is integral to the success of ROPE framework for running complex datacenter migration projects. The workstream manager, manages project segments, provides organization oversite and completes project tasks adhering to the guidance of the tower leads, program manager (project leadership) and organizational requirements.

Workstream managers possess the following skills and experience required to manage the project's communications, documentation, scheduling, budget and processes:

- Strong multi-tasking and organizational skills.
- Demonstrated willingness to be adaptable and flexible, with the ability to handle ambiguity and changing priorities.
- Demonstrated effectiveness with verbal and written communication skills.
- Demonstrated solid experience creating documentation associated with IT projects.
- Experience working with and collaborating across multiple project stakeholder groups (IT engineers, developers, analysts and business users).
- Familiarity with IT infrastructure and application development processes and methodologies.
- Comfortable administrating internal SharePoint sites.
- Experienced with project management tools (Smartsheet, MS Project).
- Experience managing medium to large IT projects.
- Experienced with Microsoft Office (Word, Excel, Power Point, Outlook) or similar office suite product.
- Proven ability to work effectively both independently as well as in a team-based environment.
- Full understanding of project management principles for both waterfall and agile methods.

Activities performed (or through direction of team members) includes:

- Develop project processes and integrate them into the enterprise's processes.
- Establish close relationship with project leadership.
- Foster a trusted working relationship with project stakeholders.
- Work with project leadership to manage / monitor /maintain deliverables and milestones defined in the project plans.
- Participate in regularly scheduled internal and external project meetings.
- Develop status and communications for project leadership and PMO.
- Lead status meetings to stakeholders.

- Perform administrative duties associated with project meetings as well as other project activities and calendaring needs.
- Organize and maintain project libraries.
- Facilitate, track and maintain purchase records.
- Track maintain and report on project budget.
- Create and maintain prescribed project management artifacts throughout the project's lifecycle.
- Assist the team with priorities, scope, budget and scheduling to ensure adherence to project goals.
- Assist project leadership in tracking project plans, work hours, budgets and expenditures.
- Maintain risk tracking and issue logs.
- Effectively and accurately communicate relevant project information to project team and stakeholders.
- Provide risk updates and escalate issues along with resolution recommendations to project leadership.
- Keep project leadership informed on all issues that may impact project goals.

Project Leader

This guide will discuss the role of the project leaders at a deeper level in a later chapter. What is important to understand at the organizational staffing level is that project leaders play a vital role in the daily execution of tasks by leading and managing the activities of multiple application moves at any one time. To be successful the project leader should have a technical background in order to develop a strong working relationship with the analysts and engineers on their teams and guide them through the ROPE framework's activities. In order to deliver results through the project team members, a project leader should possess the following skills:

- Strong multi-tasking and organizational skills.
- Demonstrated ability to manage multiple parallel projects.
- Demonstrated willingness to be adaptable and flexible, with the ability to handle ambiguity and changing priorities.
- Demonstrated effectiveness with verbal and written communication skills.
- Demonstrated experience creating and working with documentation associated with IT projects.
- Experience working with and collaborating across multiple project stakeholder groups (IT engineers, developers, analysts and business users).
- Familiarity with IT infrastructure and application development processes and methodologies.
- Familiarity with project management tools (Smart Sheet, MS Project, SharePoint sites).
- Experience successfully managing small to medium IT projects in a dynamic environment.
- Experience with Microsoft Office (Word, Excel, Power Point, Outlook) or similar office suite product.
- Proven ability to work effectively both independently as well as in a team-based environment.
- Solid understanding of traditional project management principles and methods.
- Ability to work off hours and weekends

Activities performed under the guidance and direction of the tower leads includes:

- Establish close relationship with project leadership.
- Foster a trusted working relationship with project stakeholders.
- Effectively and accurately communicate relevant project information to project team and stakeholders.

- Communicate ideas for process improvement with a positive and constructive attitude and develop this attitude in others.
- Keep project leadership informed on all issues or risks that may impact project goals
- Provide training on the ROPE framework to teams of analysts and engineers.
- Provide communications and updates to their move teams.
- Work with analysts to ensure build sheet information is complete and accurate. Work with tower leads to incorporate individual build sheet information into the build sheet master. Work with analysts to resolve data anomalies.
- Work with analysts and engineers to develop a comprehensive cut sheet for each application migration.
- Provide back up for analysts at daily huddles.
- Maintain weekly check-ins with analyst teams to proactively remove obstacles, clear up confusions, manage staffing priorities and maintain focus on the migration effort.
- Work with analysts and engineers to maintain progress against the cut sheet.
- Remove and/or escalate roadblocks facing teams working through their cut sheet.
- Ensure adherence to move train processes, coaching team members (using job aids) on how to complete tasks or engage other teams.
- Perform go/no go reviews and ensure preparedness for move event.
- Run move event and gain sign off.

RACI

The RACI provides a clear understanding of who is involved for the majority of the tasks required to move an application. The RACI is broken down by Pre-Move tasks, Move tasks and Post-Move tasks. The RACI should be reviewed and adjusted to reflect the activities and resource groups within your organization.

Who Does What

This RACI outlines the work and the roles required to move each application from old data center to new data center. The RACI is based on the build sheet, cut sheet agile move framework.

R Responsible for performing the work.

A Accountable for the work being completed.

C Contributes to the work being performed.

I Informed of the work and its completion.

Phase	Application Migration Activity	Tower Lead	Project Leader	App Analyst	QA	Business Owner	Server Engineer	Network Engineer	Security Engineer	Storage/ Backup Engineer	DBA	Vendor	Site Director/ Stake Holders	Service Desk	Workstream Manager	Service Line Leader
Pre-sprint	Create build sheet		A	R			C	C	C	C	C	C			I	
	Review build sheet with infrastructure		A	R			C	C	C	C	C	C				
	Determine move method	I	C	R		C	C	C	C	C	C	C			I	
	Approve move method	I	C	R		A										
	Determine move date	I	I	A		R						C	I/C		I	

51

Phase	Application Migration Activity	Tower Lead	Project Leader	App Analyst	QA	Business Owner	Server Engineer	Network Engineer	Security Engineer	Storage/ Backup Engineer	DBA	Vendor	Site Director/ Stake Holders	Service Desk	Workstream Manager	Service Line Leader
	Contact vendor		A	R	C							C			I	
	Determine vendor involvement		A	R	C							C				
	Develop vendor SOW		A	R	C							C			C	
	Procure vendor SOW		I	A								C			R	
	Schedule vendor participation		A	R								C			I	
	Create cut sheet tasks		A	R	C	C	C	C	C	C	C	C	C			
	Review cut sheet tasks	I	A	R	C	C	C	C	C	C	C	C			I	
Sprint pre-	Sprint Planning	I	A	R	C		C	C	C	C					C	
	Daily scrum call	A/ R	C	C	I	I	I	I	I	I	I	I	I	I	C	I
	Maintain cut sheet task list		A	R	C	C	C	C	C	C	C	C	I			

Phase	Application Migration Activity	Tower Lead	Project Leader	App Analyst	QA	Business Owner	Server Engineer	Network Engineer	Security Engineer	Storage/ Backup Engineer	DBA	Vendor	Site Director/ Stake Holders	Service Desk	Workstream Manager	Service Line Leader
	Create migration change control		A	R			I/C	I/C	I/C	I/C	I/C	I/C			C	I/C
	Develop migration communication		A	R		C							I/C		C	
	Send out migration communication (3 communications)		A	R		C							I/C	I	C	
	Update knowledge base documents		I	R								C		C	A	
	Present change at CAB		I	R			I/C	I/C	I/C	I/C	I/C	I/C			A	
	Execute pre-migration business continuity		I	A		R							I/C			
	Execute server pre-migration cut sheet tasks		I	A			R									I/C

Phase	Application Migration Activity	Tower Lead	Project Leader	App Analyst	QA	Business Owner	Server Engineer	Network Engineer	Security Engineer	Storage/ Backup Engineer	DBA	Vendor	Site Director/ Stake Holders	Service Desk	Workstream Manager	Service Line Leader
	Execute network pre-migration cut sheet tasks		I	A				R								I/C
	Execute security pre-migration cut sheet tasks		I	A					R							I/C
	Execute storage / backup pre-migration cut sheet tasks		I	A						R						I/C
	Execute DBA pre-migration cut sheet tasks		I	A							R					I/C
	Execute vendor pre-migration cut sheet tasks		I	A								R				
	Develop test plan		I	R	A	C						C	I/C			
	Perform pre-migration baseline tests		I	C	A	R						C	I/C			
	Create tech-info sheet		A	R			C	C	C	C	C	C				

Phase	Application Migration Activity	Tower Lead	Project Leader	App Analyst	QA	Business Owner	Server Engineer	Network Engineer	Security Engineer	Storage/ Backup Engineer	DBA	Vendor	Site Director/ Stake Holders	Service Desk	Workstream Manager	Service Line Leader
migration	Schedule go/no go review	I	A	R	I	I	I	I	I	I	I	I	I	I	I	
	Perform go/no go cut sheet review	A	R	C	C	C	C	C	C	C	C	C	I/C	C		
	Schedule migration conference call	I	I/C	A	I	I	I	I	I	I	I	I	I	I	R	I
	Open and run migration call	A	R	C	C	C	C	C	C	C	C	C	I/C	I		
	Maintain migration check list	A	R	C	C	C	C	C	C	C	C	C				
	Send out migration start communication	I	A	R	I	I	I	I	I	I	I	I	I	I	I	I
	Execute migration business continuity		I	A	I	R	I	I	I	I	I	I	I/C			
	Execute application migration cut sheet tasks		A	R	I	I	I	I	I	I	I	I	I			

Phase	Application Migration Activity	Tower Lead	Project Leader	App Analyst	QA	Business Owner	Server Engineer	Network Engineer	Security Engineer	Storage / Backup Engineer	DBA	Vendor	Site Director / Stake Holders	Service Desk	Workstream Manager	Service Line Leader
	Execute server migration cut sheet tasks		A	I	I	I	R	I	I	I	I	I	I			
	Execute network migration cut sheet tasks		A	I	I	I	I	R	I	I	I	I	I			
	Execute security migration cut sheet tasks		A	I	I	I	I	I	R	I	I	I	I			
	Execute storage / backup migration cut sheet tasks		A	I	I	I	I	I	I	R	I	I	I			
	Execute DBA migration cut sheet tasks		A	I	I	I	I	I	I	I	R	I	I			
	Execute vendor migration cut sheet tasks		A	I	I	I	I	I	I	I	I	R	I			
	Execute migration smoke test		A	R	I	I	I	I	I	I	I	I	I			

Phase	Application Migration Activity	Tower Lead	Project Leader	App Analyst	QA	Business Owner	Server Engineer	Network Engineer	Security Engineer	Storage/ Backup Engineer	DBA	Vendor	Site Director/ Stake Holders	Service Desk	Workstream Manager	Service Line Leader
	Execute migration test plan	I	I	A	R	I	I	I	I	I	I	I	I			
	Maintain migration issue list	A	R	C	C	C	C	C	C	C	C	C				
	Resolve migration issues		A	R		C	C	C	C	C	C	C				
	Migration go/no go		A	C	C	R	C	C	C	C	C	C	I/C			
	Execute roll back															
	Execute application rollback cut sheet tasks		A	R	I	I	I	I	I	I	I	I	I			
	Execute server rollback cut sheet tasks		A	I	I	I	R	I	I	I	I	I	I			
	Execute network rollback cut sheet tasks		A	I	I	I	I	R	I	I	I	I	I			

Phase	Application Migration Activity	Tower Lead	Project Leader	App Analyst	QA	Business Owner	Server Engineer	Network Engineer	Security Engineer	Storage / Backup Engineer	DBA	Vendor	Site Director/ Stake Holders	Service Desk	Workstream Manager	Service Line Leader
	Execute security rollback cut sheet tasks	A	I	I	I	I	I	I	R	I	I	I	I			
	Execute storage / backup rollback cut sheet tasks	A	I	I	I	I	I	I	I	R	I	I	I			
	Execute DBA rollback cut sheet tasks	A	I	I	I	I	I	I	I	I	R	I	I			
	Execute vendor rollback cut sheet tasks	A	I	I	I	I	I	I	I	I	I	R	I			
	Execute rollback smoke test	A	R	I	I	I	I	I	I	I	I	I	I			
	Execute rollback test plan	I	I	A	R	I	I	I	I	I	I	I	I	I		
	Change network monitoring system pointers							R								A

Phase	Application Migration Activity	Tower Lead	Project Leader	App Analyst	QA	Business Owner	Server Engineer	Network Engineer	Security Engineer	Storage/ Backup Engineer	DBA	Vendor	Site Director/ Stake Holders	Service Desk	Workstream Manager	Service Line Leader
	Change server monitoring system pointers						R									A
	End migration business continuity		I	A	I	R	I	I	I	I	I	I	I/C			
	Send out migration complete communication	I	A	R	I	I	I	I	I	I	I	I	I	I	I	I
	End migration call	A	R	C	C	C	C	C	C	C	C	C	I/C			
post-migration	Execute post-migration application cut sheet tasks		A	R		C							I/C	I/C	I	
	Execute server post-migration cut sheet tasks		I	A		I	R							I/C	I	
	Execute network post-migration cut sheet tasks		I	A		I		R						I/C	I	

Phase	Application Migration Activity	Tower Lead	Project Leader	App Analyst	QA	Business Owner	Server Engineer	Network Engineer	Security Engineer	Storage / Backup Engineer	DBA	Vendor	Site Director / Stake Holders	Service Desk	Workstream Manager	Service Line Leader
	Execute security post-migration cut sheet tasks	I	A			I			R					I/C	I	
	Execute storage / backup post-migration cut sheet tasks	I	A			I				R				I/C	I	
	Execute DBA post-migration cut sheet tasks	I	A			I					R			I/C	I	
	Execute vendor post-migration cut sheet tasks	I	A			I						R		I/C	I	
	Maintain post-migration cut sheet task list		A	R	I											
	Compile final documentation	I		A	C	C	C	C	C	C	C	C		R		
	Archive final documentation	I	I	I	A	I								R		
	Post migration support			A		I/C								R		
	Maintain move matrix	I	A	I	I	I	I	I	I	I	I	I	I	I	R	I

Phase	Application Migration Activity	Tower Lead	Project Leader	App Analyst	QA	Business Owner	Server Engineer	Network Engineer	Security Engineer	Storage/ Backup Engineer	DBA	Vendor	Site Director/ Stake Holders	Service Desk	Workstream Manager	Service Line Leader
	Manage server capacity	I	I				I									A/R
	Manage network capacity	I	I					I								A/R
	Manage security capacity	I	I						I							A/R
	Manage storage / backup capacity	I	I							I						A/R
	Manage database capacity	I	I								I					A/R
	Technical lessons learned	I	I	R			C	C	C	C	C	C			A	I/C
	Business lessons learned	I	I	R	C	C						C	C		A	
	Approve SOW payment	I	A	C								I/C			R	

61

Role	Description
Tower Lead	Leader over all workstream activities under their given tower.
Project Leader	Leads and manages multiple application moves.
System Analyst	Technical owner of the application. This is the person is responsible for the day to day care and feed of the application from a technical perspective.
QA	Enterprise quality assurance group representative assigned to an application
Business Owner	The business owner (or their designate) represents the interests of the individuals using the application. This is the person who would approve committing dollars and resources to an upgrade.
Architect	Bridges technology groups and knows the processes that allow the various groups to function together.
Server Engineer	Engineer responsible for the care and feeding of compute resources (Windows, Unix, Linux). Dedicated to the move of an application.
Network Engineer	Engineer responsible for the care and feeding of network resources across the enterprise. Dedicated to the move of an application.
Storage / Backup Engineer	Engineer responsible for the care and feeding of storage / backup resources. Dedicated to the move of an application.
DBA	Database analyst responsible for the care and feeding of database resources (MS SQL Oracle, Sybase) Dedicated to the move of an applications database or shared database resource.
Vendor	Provider of an application. May have maintenance contract. Application may run on a black box/ grey box service. May need a separate contract or SOW for the work to move the application.
Site Director	Responsible for oversight of all activities at a patient care, plant floor, or major business location or group.

Service Desk	Internal and external customer contact for technical issues escalation and resolution support. Available 7x24. May be referred to as the NOC or operations center.
Tech Ops / Command Center	Monitors technology providing tier 1 support and incident escalation. Available 7x24. May be referred to as the NOC.
Workstream Manager	Supports the teams moving an application.
Service Line Leader	Manager of infrastructure engineering resources responsible for operations of their technical area.

Communication plan

A datacenter migration is one of the most complex and far reaching projects an enterprise will initiate. Over its life it will affect everyone in the organization. Poor project communication will cause unnecessary chaos and confusion throughout the organization.

A good communication plan is your road map for getting your project's message delivered to your audience. It's an essential tool for ensuring your datacenter migration project sends a clear, specific message with transparency as the goal.

Over the years the following communication plan has provided an effective method for communicating project status and informing stakeholders across the organization. The intent with communication is transparency and the project team should strive to always pass along clear, concise and accurate information in all communication.

Involvement	Description	Who	M	W	D
Program Steering Board	Provide overall budget state, progress status and risks. Request strategic guidance, support and message amplification.	• Executive sponsor • Steering board members • Program owner • Program manager • Tower leads • Workstream manager	X		
Program Advisory Board	Provide overall state, progress status and risks. Request strategic guidance, support and message amplification. May initially start out as every other week.	• Program owner • Advisory board members • Program manager • Tower leads • Workstream manager	X		
Program Owner Update	Review detailed budget state, progress status, issues, risks and	• Program owner		X	

Involvement	Description	Who	M	W	D
	mitigation recommendations. Request guidance and support. Request guidance on organizational issues.	• Program manager • Tower leads • Workstream manager			
Application / Infrastructure Managers Update	Review overall progress status and risks. Request support and guidance.	• Managers • Tower leads • Workstream manager		X	
Project Team Group Up	A forward-looking meeting to ensure all workstreams are in synch. Discuss issues. Request tactical guidance and peer support.	• Program manager • Tower leads • Workstream manager • Project leaders		X	
Move Team Check-In	Keep analyst teams and infrastructure teams up to date on program. Discuss upcoming moves. Provide guidance and support. Tie into tech teams' existing meetings.	• Project leader • Application / service technical owner		X	
Sprint Planning	Discuss applications starting the move process. Ensure all infrastructure teams know what is required. Ensure analyst understands what is required.	• All active project contributors		X	
Application Move Huddle	Daily check-in on application move progress once an application enters sprint process.	• All active project contributors			X

Involvement	Description	Who	M	W	D
	Opportunity to escalate any issues or concerns.				
Status Report	Summary of work across the program. Includes budget state, progress and risks	• PPMO • All stakeholders		X	
Dash Board	Real-time, interactive report of work across the program. Maintained in Smartsheet	• All stakeholders			X
Town Halls	As needed to convey significant topic to large audience and receive feedback or input	• All stakeholders			
FAQ	Maintain document of questions and answers. Reference and distribute link (off of dashboard) to ensure consistent answers across all groups and provide self-service information.	• All stakeholders			

Your organization may require additional reporting to meet PMO requirements. We have found that meeting PMO requirements is relatively straightforward for the workstream manager to complete by reformatting information available in the project's status report and dashboard.

Risk Management

Building a new datacenter and moving all of the applications and services from one datacenter to another is inherently high risk. In a datacenter migration project, risk takes on many forms including:

- Procurement processes take significantly longer than planned due to amount of costs or architectural changes.
- Construction and tenant improvement dates slip.
- IT Equipment is back logged from the vendor/manufacturer.
- Missed IT equipment components (fiber/copper, optics, drives, ...) on initial orders requiring additional spend and time.
- Network circuit order lead times exceed planned deliver times or incomplete delivery from the circuit provider delays deployments.
- New IT Infrastructure configuration times exceed plan due to unexpected complexity.
- End to end IT infrastructure tests may not test every possible case due to the endless number of edge cases.
- Technical debt within the old datacenter is significant.
- Changing security requirements to combat new or evolving threats.
- Changing business drivers, budget or executive leadership.
- Insufficient staffing levels, changes to staffing assignments and/or staff reductions.
- Competing priorities for assigned resources.
- Incomplete knowledge of applications and/or services.
- Orphan applications (apps without a technical owner).
- Unknown customer impacts of application/service outages.
- Non-IT supported items (Access DB, managed services, underground IT systems...) in production.
- Organizational politics conflict with project goal.
- Organizational culture resistant to change.
- Physical systems break, networks crash, routes are lost, and spinning disks stop.

Even the best plans cannot remove all the risks associated with a datacenter migration, but it can be managed. The ROPE framework manages risk and provides visibility to leadership through the use of the RAIDq. The RAIDq is a simple Smartsheet grid designed to maintain critical information about key project Risks, Actions, Issues, Decisions, Question.

The project team reviews the RAIDq weekly with the project owner to ensure items are being managed or escalated appropriately. Decisions and actions are kept in order to ensure outcomes can be walked back to their origins. Often the decisions are the outcome from steering board meeting guidance requests.

The RAIDq has the following columns:

Column Heading	Description
Resolved	Check box to indicate the item is no longer a concern. This check box is only associated with risks and issues
RAIDq	A pull down to indicate if the item is a: risk, action, issue, decision or question
Priority	A graphical pull down indicating high, medium or low priority (importance).
Title	Short description of the item.
Description	Complete information about the item. Should give any reader a full understanding of the item.
Resolution	The resulting outcome or actions taken for the item. In the case of a risk this should be the mitigation plan.
Date Entered	Date the item was entered into the RAIDq. If you are using Smartsheet this can be a system generated item.
Next Check In	What date should this item be revisited. A Smartsheet comment should be created for the item row anytime it is checked on. Smartsheet comments will automatically date and timestamp the comment as well as note who entered it, helping the team manage and track the item.
Last Updated	Date of last action. If you are using Smartsheet this can be a system generated item.
Date Resolved	Date the item no longer requires attention or action.

The key to successful RAIDq management is keeping the log visible in order to maintain leadership focus. To maintain visibility, the RAIDq is reported prominently on the dashboard. Review of the RAIDq should be an agenda item on the following meetings:

- Program owner's weekly update
- Application / Infrastructure Managers Update
- Program Advisory Board meeting
- Program Steering Board meeting

Risk and issues should always be accompanied with mitigations and actions being taken. Continued updates need to be added to ensure progress on eliminating the risk or issue until the issue is resolved or the risk has passed.

One important distinction is that there are hundreds of risks and issues faced on complex technology projects. The RAIDq contains only those items that the project management team wants to ensure visibility, awareness and support from leadership. The remaining lower level risks and issues are brought up and resolved daily by the project team through the activities of the ROPE framework such as daily huddles, group up, check ins and escalation to the tower leads for resolution.

Generally, we set up a format rule in Smartsheet for the RAIDq that will highlight items based on the next check in date. The highlight is applied to rows a few days before the next check-in to ensure item follow-up is not missed.

Change Control

The "Move Method Options" document provides options in the form of standard move choices for analysts and/or business owners to select from that will meet their needs. It also sets boundaries for changes that can occur within the move process such as a "Like for Like" move. The options and boundaries are intended to balance the need for flexibility with the requirement to complete the project on time, maintain velocity and manage scope. When analysts and/or business owners find themselves desiring a non-standard approach or a significant change to the approach, the ROPE frameworks provides a process to govern change.

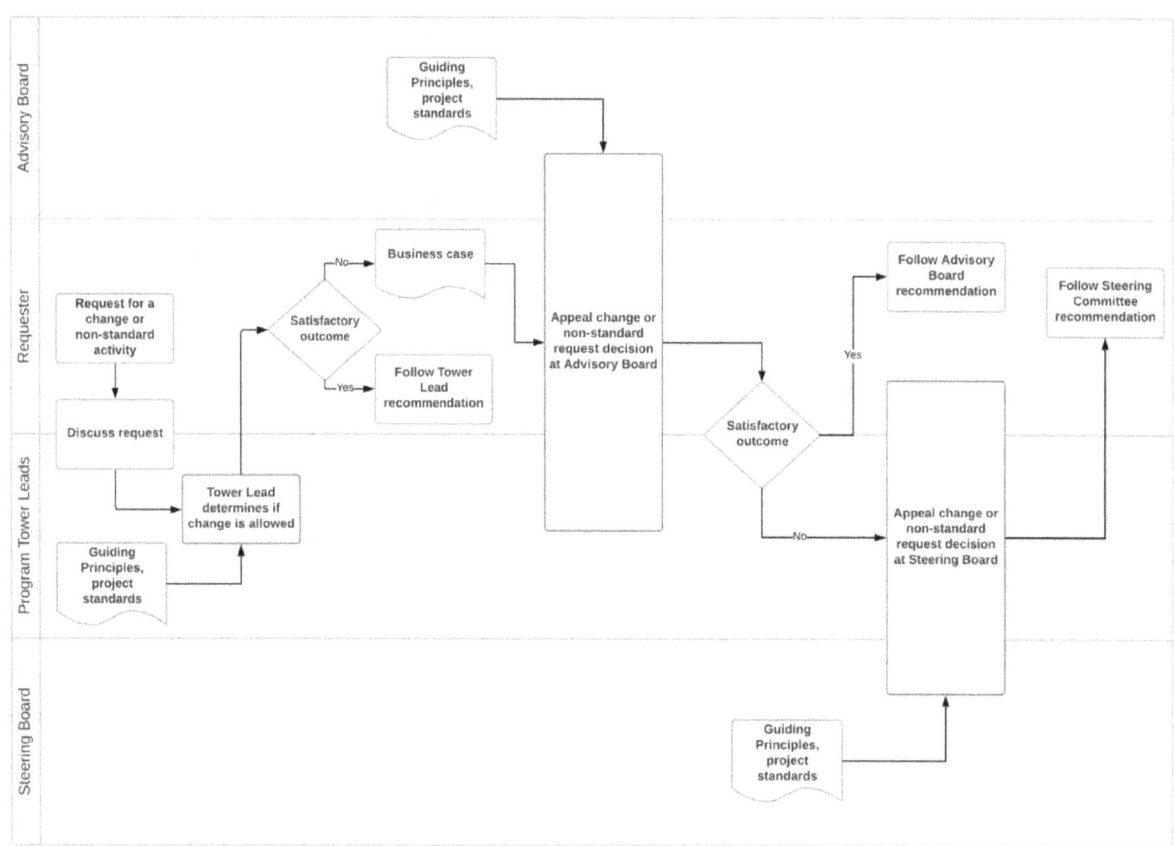

The initial change request is a conversation between the requester and the tower lead where they can discuss the benefits, risks, impacts and rewards of the change. Using the guiding principles, her experience and an understanding of the impacts that the change will have on the project, the tower lead will accept or reject a change request and explain why their decision is appropriate. The two tower leads may consult together but the tower lead who's workstream is involved will make the decision.

More often than not the decision will be to reject the change request. The reason for defaulting to a rejected change is because the standard move options already provides significant leeway for moving and the guiding principles driving the project have been applied to the processes governing the move options. Additionally, the tower lead is evaluating the change against the entire project while the requester is often focused on their individual application. As discussed earlier, left unchecked, short sighted changes or over optimizing individual application moves leads to the "death by 1,000 cuts" syndrome.

The goal of the project is to move the datacenter and changes that detract from that goal must provide a significant return on investment.

If the requester is unsatisfied with the tower lead's decision, they may choose to appeal and present a formal written business case justification to the advisory board. The advisory board will review the request, listen to the consultation of the tower lead and look for guidance from the guiding principles in order to accept or reject the change request.

If the requester is unsatisfied with the advisory board's decision, they may choose to appeal and present their formal written business case justification to the steering board. The steering board will review the request, listen to the consultation of the tower lead and evaluate it against the guiding principles they set forth to the project in order to accept or reject the change request. The steering board's decision is final.

The steering board may choose to review any decision made by the advisory board without an appeal from the requestor if they feel the guiding principles have been misinterpreted or wish to set direction for similar future change requests.

Migration Process Training

Material Overview

The datacenter move training material is focused on moving applications and data because at the end of the day it is the applications and their data that run the business, not the servers, switches or spinning disk. We often compare this to a washer and dryer. A properly functioning washer and dryer is critical to ensure the water temperature is correct, the soap and fabric softener are distributed evenly, and a constant flow of warm air removes the moisture and wrinkles. However, without a pile of dirty clothes, there is little need for the hardware.

One component of successful moves is ensuring everyone involved goes through the training so that they have the same understanding of the ROPE framework as it applies to this datacenter migration and the expectation placed of the team members in the process. We find the training most successful when presented in the following order:

1. Steering board and advisory board.
2. Infrastructure managers and leaders.
3. Infrastructure engineers as a whole.
4. Application Managers and leaders whose staff are responsible for the technical support of applications.
5. Application analysts, DBAs, operations and other support groups by logical application support grouping. For example: in healthcare this grouping may be around Clinical support, back office, imaging, ...

This material has been presented to multiple organizations of various sizes across several different industries. The material should be considered a base-level. Changes and additions to the deck should be made to convey the specific information you need for your datacenter migration project.

The training session along with Q&A should take one to one and a half hours for each group. The assumption of the training is that training is the first exposure to the material. Project leaders and tower leads will reinforce the concepts and activities as they work with the teams throughout the process.

Slide 1 Datacenter Migration Training

DATACENTER
MIGRATION
TRAINING

Keys To A Successful Approach
Leadership, Priority and Communication

The cover slide provides the presenter an opportunity to set the context for this project. Use this slide as an opportunity to discuss the following:

- Why the datacenter is moving (consolidation of resources, removing risk associated with an older datacenter, growth and expansion, ...) and how they will be better served once the datacenter migration is complete.
- Explain the priority leadership has given the project within the organization and reinforce that the datacenter move project tasks will need to take precedence over other work.
- Highlight to everyone that clear communication with stakeholders is key to avoiding problems. Email is great, but an unanswered email needs to be followed up with more personal communication methods. A theme throughout the ROPE framework is clear, consistent communication.

Slide 2 Migration Training Topics

MIGRATION TRAINING TOPICS
How to successfully move your application with the least amount of work

Principles
What's Different

Tools
Few and Effective

Process
The Migration Methodology

Next Steps
Your Involvement

Slide 2 allows the presenter to set the stage for what will be covered in the training. Some individuals may have participated in datacenter move projects in the past. It is important to recognize that experience and explain that the ROPE framework and processes you're going to cover may approach it differently. Emphasize there are many ways to move a datacenter, but leadership has agreed this is how the enterprise will perform this datacenter migration project.

Slide 3 Agile Micro Move Framework

The results oriented project execution framework is a flexible, iterative approach that minimizes business stress, maintains schedule momentum and delivers success without loosing visibility, quality or control.

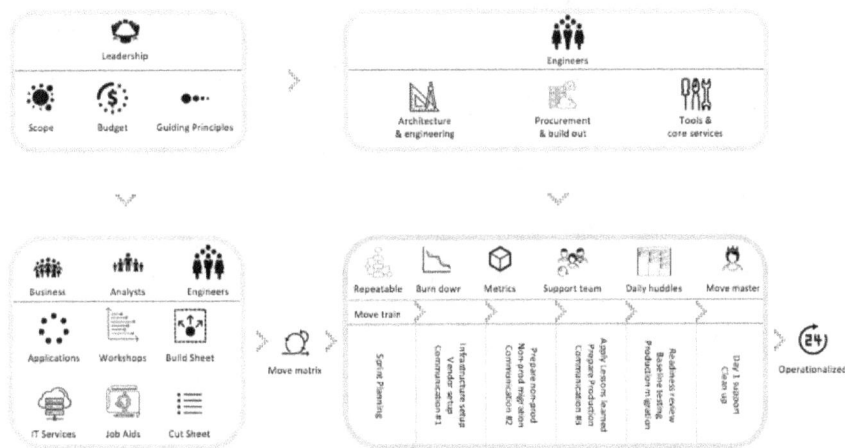

Explain the overall framework at a high-level. The framework has four key aspects: Leadership Guidance, Engineering Build, Discovery and Planning, and the Move Train.

It is important to emphasize leadership's involvement. Often the decision to move the datacenter has been ratified at the board level to ensure funding, priority and commitment. Make sure everyone understands the level of commitment behind the project.

Unless the training is being given to the infrastructure teams, it is likely most of the audience is unfamiliar with many of the specifics of the new datacenter. At a high-level explain where the new datacenter is located and highlight any significant improvements planned for implementation. Improvements may include faster storage and compute platforms, faster more secure networks or expansion capabilities to meet projected business growth.

The Discovery and Planning as well as the Move Train will be the bulk of the discussion that the training will cover. Before leaving this slide, you may want to point out:

- The Discovery and Planning as well as the Move Train involve all stakeholders. The project will require application analysts, engineers and business staff to collaborate in order for the migration to be successful.
- While applications and services may seem different, they will be treated the same from the perspective of how their move will be managed.

- The framework uses an agile approach and for some, there will be an uncomfortable feeling of ambiguity at times. However, as an application progresses through the process, required details and clarity are added as needed to ensure a successful outcome.
- The Move Train will be covered in more detail, but one of the reasons it is set at four weeks is so that stakeholder communication can be sent out 3 weeks, 2 weeks and one week prior to the move in order to provide lead time and ensure delivery to stakeholders who may want reminders. It also allows for change ticket reviews and change board approval times which in some organizations can have lengthy process durations.

Slide 4 Program Boundaries

PROGRAM BOUNDARIES

Managing scope is key to success. Over reaching on scope is the most common mistake

In Scope

Equipment
Equipment in Canton datacenter or floor space under lease

Applications
Applications and services delivered from Canton datacenter

Datacenter Processes
Process functions need to continue. For example: monitoring

Connectivity
WAN circuits, partner circuits, third-party access points

Facility
Facility meets turnover requirement

Out of Scope

Operational support processes	Application upgrades or changes	Application rationalization	Operating system upgrades
Data center lifecycle efforts	Active Directory consolidation	Client upgrades or changes not related to application move	Database upgrades or changes
Hardware upgrades or changes	Server standardization or non-required improvements	Equipment not in old data center	Disaster recovery

Scope is important for everyone to understand. Scope explains where the boundaries of the project lie. This slide should be updated to reflect the scope of your datacenter migration project. The final version of this slide should be vetted with the projects sponsor and senior leadership to ensure buy-in. The scope slide should be a reflection of your project charter.

As you can see in this example there are more out of scope items than in scope. We have found that clearly calling out what is not in scope is more effective than drilling down into categories such as applications and listing all applications in scope. That drill down is found in the Move Matrix where every application and service have a line item.

Clearly identify and discuss out of scope items that can easily lead to scope creep such as upgrades, disaster recovery improvements, or desktop improvements. The point to emphasize when presenting this slide is that the is project is focused on migrating the datacenter, not repaying all the technical debt that has accumulated over the years.

Slide 5 Guiding Principles

GUIDING PRINCIPLES

The principles, guide what we do, why we do it and how. Our principles serve as guardrails for making decisions in pursuit of our goal: To Move Out of the Datacenter

Cloud First
AWS is the strategic direction from our leadership

Aha Moment,
The datacenter migration is an Application Project

App Teams Got This
App analysts own the migration, Infrastructure teams support them

Like for Like
Keep applications, technology and user experience consistent

Mind The Risk
Small manageable moves are low risk to our business and customers

Keep it Repeatable
Use what works until it doesn't then only make small tweaks

Involve Me
Stakeholders actively engaged and awareness is apparent

Decide and Move On
Consider the data, decide and continue, don't dwell on it

As mentioned before, guiding principles are one of the most powerful tools senior leadership can provide to the datacenter migration project. This slide should be updated to reflect your negotiated guiding principles. The guiding principles sets the tone for project, allowing tower leads and project leaders to drive the datacenter migration project with the backing of senior leadership.

In the training explain that leadership has given these guiding principles to the datacenter migration project to drive decisions down through the project leaders. Review each of the principles and explain what that principle means to the project. For example: "Like for Like" allows the project to move applications that may not be within current standard knowing that following the move, application analysts may need to plan an upgrade to their application.

Slide 6 Principles in Practice

PRINCIPLES IN PRACTICE
How we apply leadership's guidance

Target Completion is June 20XX

"Like-for-Like"	"Keep it Repeatable"	"Manageable Risk"	"We Got This"
Upgrades: The *answer is "No"*	V2V or Build New or AWS	One application at a time	By "We", we mean you!
Destination AWS or new datacenter – your choice	Choice based on risk, effort and outage tolerance	Big waves increase complexity, risk and makes it harder than it has to be	We'll coach you through it, following the process is not that hard

Slide 6 allows you to call out specific guiding principles that you may want to reiterate. We typically select those guiding principles that are non-standard to the organization culture or need to be emphasized for understanding.

Use slide 5 and slide 6 to solidify with everyone that senior leadership is fully supporting the datacenter move project, its priority and that the ROPE framework and its processes are driving the project.

Slide 7 RACI

RACI

Clearly defined roles with the right individual performing the right tasks.

Responsible	Accountable	Consult	Inform
I got it!	*The buck stops here.*	*Subject matter expert*	*Let me know*
Individual tasked with completing the work	Individual is answerable for the work completion	Provides insights and guidance about completing the work	Receives status on task progress and/or completion

RACI Matrix - <link to RACI goes here> 7

The RACI provides two key pieces of information. The first is the typical roles and responsibilities. During the training we use this opportunity to emphasize that unlike some projects, the ROPE framework assigns most of the accountability and responsibility for task completion to team members rather than the project leaders. This shift is in line with most agile frameworks where individuals on the team make commitments and are held accountable for meeting those commitments. It also associates tasks with multiple steps to the individual most equipped to own them, removing the overhead and added handoff delays inherent to more waterfall-oriented projects. If the tasks present too large of a burden on individuals, you may want to add coordinators or administrative support to supplement the team.

The second value of the detailed RACI is that it provides a solid outline for most of the tasks that will be required to move each application. Analysts and engineers can utilize the RACI as a starting point for their task list and then adjust their task lists for anything that may be unique to the organization and individual application.

At some point in this slide's discussion, click on the RACI Matrix link and quickly roll though it to show the audience it's depth and availability.

Slide 8 Agile Tools

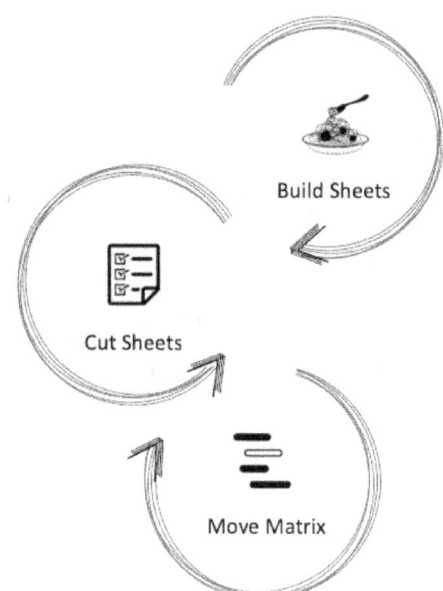

AGILE TOOLS
Minimizes documentation while maximizing the results

- WHAT: Build Sheets define an application, its systems, data stores and interfaces
- HOW: Cut Sheets layout the prep work, steps executed during the cutover, testing and post migration clean up. A back-out plan is built just in case.
- WHEN: Move Matrix tracks where an application is in the process, key milestones and who owns it.

Build Sheets

Cut Sheets

Move Matrix

Slide 8 starts the discussion of what and how the discovery and planning will occur. This slide also ties back to the ROPE framework showing the flow of the build sheets, cut sheets and move matrix.

The build sheets show the current As-Is state (requirements) of the application. This includes documenting the various components such as web front-ends, applications and databases as well as the servers and IP addresses associated with the application. Build sheets also document the application's interfaces, those other applications, services and databases this application talks to in order for a user to complete their workflow.

Once the As-Is state is known for an application, the analysts and team are ready to move onto the cut sheet which will establish the steps needed to move the application to its To-Be state in the new datacenter.

The move matrix is the schedule for application moves. Within the move matrix there is a row for each application and service along with its associated move date. Since the driving assumption is that applications are free to move independent of other applications, individual applications can be scheduled to move when it is best for the customer. If there is truly tight coupling between applications requiring multiple applications to move together, each application in the move matrix should have the same move date and their cut sheet activities synchronized. This will allow individual application focus while maintaining the relationship between the tightly coupled applications.

As the arrows indicate, occasionally in the process of developing the cut sheet or as the move matrix develops, new information will be discovered that needs to be fed back into the build sheet or the cut sheet. This is a natural part of the iterative process.

Slide 9 Tools That Work

TOOLS THAT WORK
Focus work and effort where it will deliver the best results

Build Sheet

Minimal "AS IS" info needed

Think spaghetti: connections, interfaces – what is attached to your app that needs to move or change

list of application interdependencies

Cut Sheet

Check list style migration plan to execute against

Week-by-week prep tasks

Minute-by-minute cutover steps

Back-out plan and contacts

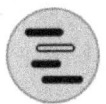

Move Matrix

Spread sheet with critical dates for each application

Sprint planning, non-prod and production moves

Move planning and resource planning

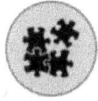

Smart Sheet

Project management tool for non-project manager

One place for all info

Focus on execution, document only the essentials

Slide 9 reiterates the build sheet, cut sheet and move matrix. It also introduces Smartsheet (smartsheet.com).   If this project is introducing Smartsheet to your organization, it is important to discuss with everyone the need to use Smartsheet over Excel or other spreadsheet tools when they capture or exchange information. The collaborative value of Smartsheet and version control over standard spreadsheets is critical to a fast-paced technology project.

An important piece of information and one of the hardest to gather for the build sheet are the interfaces. Interfaces are typically where problems occur when moving an application. By documenting them in the build sheet, analysts are creating the core of their test plan. Once the application is moved, all the interfaces need to be tested in order to know the application is working correctly in its new location.

At this point bring up a build sheet and discuss each field and why it is collected. Explain how the analysts access and fill out a build sheet for each of their applications.

One question that often comes up when explaining the build sheet is: "can I put all my applications on one build sheet?"

The answer is: "You want one application per build sheet. This keeps the information for each application segmented to one group of sheets. It also allows for easier reviews and QA of the information as well as providing interface tests on an application by application basis. This does not mean multiple applications can't move together, but each will have their own build sheet to ensure the details are fully captured"

The cut sheet lists all the tasks needed to perform the move. Bring up a cut sheet as you discuss its use and content with the audience.

The pre-move tasks include submitting change controls, sending out communications, lowering the TTL for DNS, and so on. These tasks are basic with additional detail that is unique for the application such as data synchronization or license key requirements or identifying configuration changes for new IP and host names. For the actual move event, every step will need to be documented so that nothing is missed that might cause an outage. This includes a step for shutting down each component of the application in correct order, which configuration file is being modified by who, changing the out of band IP address, updating DNS, and so on. Some tasks may be required Post-move. These are generally cleanup tasks and tend to be the same for most applications. Post-move tasks may include: kicking off a new backup, setting the DNS TTL back to its default, closing out change control and so on. All these tasks are captured in the cut sheet for an individual application.

You'll see that the move matrix is broken into three parts: "In Process" are the applications actively going through the move train, "Back Log" are applications waiting to join the move train and "Complete" are applications that have moved and signed off.

At this point bring up the Move Matrix and show how it flows.

A common question that comes up around the move matrix is: "What if I need to move my application the same day and time as someone else?"

The answer is: "This will often be the case. Frequently move event windows are set for the same or overlapping times. The process allows for moves to happen at the same time because you can look at each individual move's build sheet and cut sheet to quickly identify any conflicts. By having individual cut sheets each move event can be run in parallel as a standalone activity. In fact, on one conference call we may be running multiple move events at any one time, because we have the cut sheet that has scripted out the tasks ahead of time, everyone knows what they are doing when."

When we work with teams, we often use the phrase "less is more". This phrase is meant to remind everyone to focus on what is important for the job at hand and to let go of things that are not advancing the project. A good example of this follows:

At one engagement, we took over their datacenter migration project from a team that had been in place for several years. Over that time the project managers and technical team had collected every possible piece of information about applications, server assignments, storage capacity, port counts, OS patch levels, application renewal dates, and just about everything else possible to know about the environment. Yet they had not moved a single application.

The team was worried, thinking they needed to know everything, before they could do anything. Unfortunately, changes are happening across the enterprise on a daily basis and data captured was out of date. Our approach using the ROPE framework is to empower the engineers and analysts to do their job. Do engineers need to keep track of port counts, capacity and all the technology aspects of their job? Yes, and engineers have access to the technical information they need when they need it. If it does not impact the scheduling of the move, engineers will bring that information into the cut sheet conversations or access the information as required to perform their tasks. They should however be reviewing all the information in their domain on a regular basis, so they can call out specific items they may need to perform or collaborate on during the development and execution of the cut sheet.

The phrase less is more applies to the all three of these tools. The build sheet is focused on the bits of information necessary to ensure everyone is speaking about the same thing and the interfaces are identified so that the spider web of connectivity is understood by all. The move matrix is focused on dates: when does the application come into planning, when do the lower environments move, when are communications going out and when is the application moving.

Even the cut sheet which is the most detailed sheet allows for analysts and engineers to do their work without telling them how to do their job. A good understanding for setting the appropriate detail in the cut sheet can be found in the book "The Checklist Manifesto: How to Get Things Right" by Atul Gawande (Author). The goal of the cut sheet is to make sure everything that needs to get done is completed in the right order without transcribing every command that an engineer or analyst will have to enter. If that level of detail is required by an engineer, they should develop a MOP (method of procedure) and key tasks from the MOP can be brought back into the cut sheet.

The build sheet, cut sheet and move matrix are built in Smartsheet[5]. We often refer to Smartsheet as "project management for non-project managers". Think checklists, punch lists or lists of information to gather and complete. While you can perform a datacenter migration following the ROPE framework using Excel and SharePoint, we do not recommend it. The ROPE framework encourages collaboration. Smartsheet is built to facilitate collaboration and is optimized for managing projects collaboratively. Additionally, Smartsheet provides for real-time rollup reporting through interactive dashboards. Throughout this guide we assume you are using Smartsheet.

---

[5] www.smartsheet.com third party tool provided as a SAAS solution

Slide 10 Comb Through the Complexity

COMB THROUGH THE COMPLEXITY

Small manageable moves lower the impact to business staff and customers. Key to making it manageable is understanding complexity and mitigating the risk it poses

Mind the Interfaces

How is the application tied to other applications and data bases

Where and how do clients access the application

Shared server

What else is on the server

Is there a shared database involved

Timing is everything

How much outage can the business and staff accept

Break down the work

Which servers have to move together and why

10

Slide 10 explains how analysts can begin to remove the complexity of moving their application and begin filling in the build sheet, cut sheet and move matrix.

As analysts begin to fill in their build sheets, they need to pay attention to the interfaces. More post-move issues are the result of missed connections than anything else. It is particularly important to identify any connections external clients may have through VPN, jump boxes or other devices where firewall rules must be considered and setup prior to the move. When identifying server to server connections, analysts only need to go to the next hop. They do not need to document the full path of communication for their entire workflow. For example:

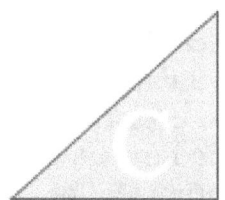

If application "A" connects to interface engine "B" in order to talk with database "C":

- Analyst for application "A" will document "B" as its interface.
- Analyst for interface engine "B" will document "A" and "C" as its interfaces.

84

- Analyst for database "C" will document "B" as its interface.

The reason for settling on this level of interface documentation is that when "A" moves "C" should not require changes or testing. Both "A" and "C" are affected when "B" changes and "B" will need to be tested as "C" moves.

A shared server exists when two or more different applications or databases reside on the same server. Shared servers present a challenge in that when the server is moved all applications are moved. If the applications sharing a server can be moved together then the steps for moving the server must include all steps associated with all applications and their interfaces. If all the applications on a server cannot be moved at the same time, applications will need to be moved off the server and onto their own server in order to break the server dependency. This is typically completed by installing the applications on new servers and migrating them following a build new process which then becomes a dependency that must be completed before the shared server and its remaining applications can move. This dependency should be watched closely as the build new process can be lengthy depending on organizational requirements.

As discussed in the standard move document there are typically four options (your organization will have to decide which will be supported with the goal being to limit options to the minimum required). In addition to covering the basic move options, the standard move document lays out the down times, risks and effort (planning documentation) required. If an application is running on a high-end physical server (expensive) and cannot take the downtime required to physically move, a build new move is probably the correct option, but it will have additional costs for hardware and software as well as all the time and effort required to install, test and synch the application on the new hardware.

"Break down the work" refers to creating the cut sheet and developing a check list of steps that will need to be completed prior to the move event, during the move event and then any follow up post-move tasks. Break the work up into bite size pieces without going down to every pebble on the beach. "The Checklist Manifesto" by Atul Gawande is a good resource to assist in achieving the appropriate level of detail.

Slide 11 Basics of Moving an Application

BASICS OF MOVING AN APPLICATION

Analysts (technical application owners) are the best qualified individuals to migrate their applications.

Business

Determine best date and time for the move (avoid maintenance windows)

Discuss outage limits

Consider business continuity during move

Standard move options

V2V or Build New or AWS

Job aid covering the details on each option

Get help

Discuss options with your PM

QA help with testing

Job aids

Build sheet & cut sheet

Highlight servers, interfaces and connectivity

Organize pre-work, migration work & post-work

Slide 11 reinforces what we've discussed. Involve the business by collaborating with them on a date and time that will work best for them to move and test the application. Early in the project, the date may be stated as any Wednesday or the second week of the month or even September after the back to school rush. You are initially looking to begin the conversation and prepare the business for their role in the move.

Over time, keep refining the move date until you have a specific date and time. This specification should become apparent through on-going conversations. The sooner you have solid dates and times set for all the individual moves the sooner you will have a schedule of back log items you can drive too. Additionally, move dates for all the applications will bring visibility to any conflicts or resource constraints as well as identify overly aggressive scheduling areas of concern. We strongly encourage teams to schedule their application move sooner than later. Scheduling application moves toward the end leaves no room for rescheduling if a business conflict arises.

Remember for best results involve the business performing the testing sign off. This involvement is important for the business to understand as you negotiate the time of day for the move. They will need to schedule staff to participate in the move event.

As mentioned before, keep the moves standard. The reasons for any individual move to be different are numerous and logical but over optimizing individual moves is done at the peril of the overall datacenter migration project. Don't let your datacenter migration project die a death of 1,000 cuts.

Project leaders should start having check-ins with teams as they get started. This will be essential to ensure build sheets are filled in consistently as well as answer questions from all the stakeholders. As an application gets closer to the move date, meet more frequently to review and refine the cut sheet to ensure progress is being made for all the pre-move tasks as well as ensure every step of the move event has been considered and assigned.

Slide 12 Consider Your Move

CONSIDER YOUR MOVE
Keep an open mind and remain flexible in considering how to move an application

 Think simplicity and stay flexible when considering options

 Servers can communicate across data centers allowing more complex applications to migrate in several small moves

Knowing server interfaces and user access are key to testing

 IP address and hostname will change

Take advantage of load balancing if possible

 Consider moving servers attached to interface engine or with large number of interfaces separately to focus testing and limit change.

Slide 12 reinforces many of the points built on throughout this training. Knowing the application/server interfaces is key to ensuring a successful move and lays out what needs to be tested.

Any application with a large number of interfaces presents a higher level of complexity. Moving it alone allows debugging efforts to remain focused.

If load balancing is used by the application, consider breaking up the application into a few smaller moves that allows load balancing to shift the work and reduce the amount of downtime required.

Simplicity is key. Avoid over complicating a move by attempting heroic technical efforts to remove an hour of downtime. Often your customer will be willing to absorb the planned downtime to reduce the overall risk introduced by technology complexity. Discuss the risk and the benefit with them. Remember you may save an hour for one application but at the cost of dozens of other application moves that must wait until resources are free.

Slide 14 Definition of Done

DEFINITION OF DONE
How do you know you're ready. How do you know you're done

Ready	Go	Done
Move date and window set	Move cutover tasks complete	Post-move work complete
Build sheet complete	Application tested	Decommission tickets closed
Cut sheet tasks defined	Sign-off received	
Pre-move work complete	Operational hand-off complete	
Cut sheet reviewed by all participants, "go" received		

Slide 13 emphasizes the importance of done. There are three gates:

1. Ready to move an application.
2. Moving an application.
3. Cleaning up and accounting for the application move.

An application is ready to move when all the pre-move steps are complete, and the move has received a "go" from all stakeholders. A formal review of the cut sheet should be held a few days prior to the move event. During the review, walk through any uncompleted pre-move steps to ensure they will be completed or that they are no longer necessary. Walk through step by step the actual event tasks. Everyone must agree all the steps are accounted for, in the correct order and assigned to the proper person. Once everyone agrees and gives their "go" the application is ready to move.

Moving an application is a coordinated execution of the steps in the cut sheet with all the actors on a call. See "Move Event under Role of The Project Leader" for specifics. At the end of the move, all the actors need to give their "go" indicating the move is complete and operational support is now responsible for issues going forward. The "go" may be conditional such as "need to have the printers rebooted in the morning" or "modalities need to have IP changes performed as called out in the post-move step". A "no go" would indicate requiring a roll back.

The final "Done" step is to take care of any post-move items. This may include updating monitoring systems, adjusting backups, or documenting change control as well as completing any decommission work required to clean up the application, server(s), load balancing VIPs or other services used in the old datacenter. Think of an application as being done when it "leaves no trace" in the old datacenter.

Slide 14 Field of Play In A Move

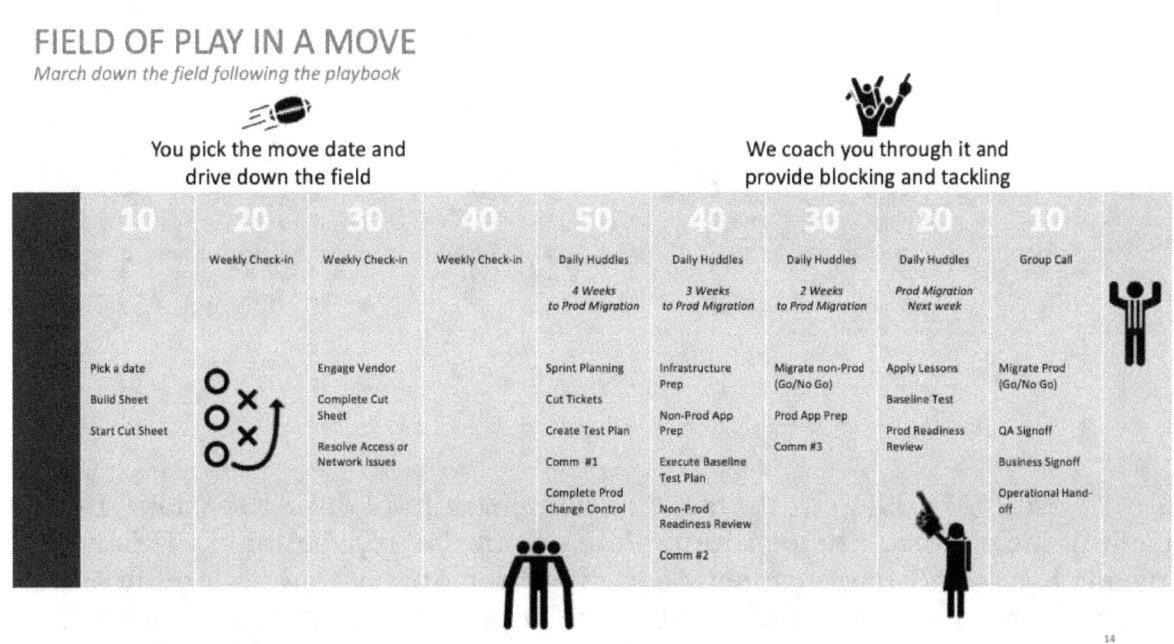

Because the ROPE framework is different than a standard water fall approach slide 14 offers a different perspective of the path each application will follow. The key is to understand that each application will run the length of the field independently. All applications should start the data gathering process together in order to complete their build sheets at the same time, but they will sprint from the 50-yard line to the goal when the rhythm of the business dictates.

Although applications move independently, those applications that interface (communicate) to applications moving will be called in to test. Applications with large numbers of interfaces such as a middleware component that routes communications, will be a part of many moves' test plan. This process will be repeated for each move event until all applications are migrated.

Explain how the first set of applications to go through the move train will be treated as pilot moves. Ten to 20 low risk applications will be selected by the application analysts and business owners to test out the move train process and overall assumptions.

Slide 15 Sprint Planning

SPRINT PLANNING

Bringing the application and infrastructure teams' knowledge together

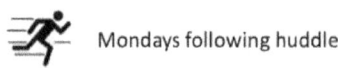 Mondays following huddles

 Tell the story

What makes this application great

Where are users and how do they access

What data is kept (PCI)

Is a vendor involved (black / grey box)

Talk about the servers (#, web, app, DB, Prod/non-Prod)

How will it be moved and tested

Sprint planning is different than a traditional scrum planning session. In this case it is the opportunity to ground all teams in the applications. This is typically a 15 to 20-minute discussion about the application, its architecture and its usage. We have found that the sprint planning discussion brings to light many hidden bits of institutional knowledge about the application.

This is the opportunity for engineers to ask general questions to determine if further discussions will be required to build out specific details in the cut sheet. If applications are moving into security zones, this discussion allows security engineers to determine and assign the application to a specific zone and start their firewall rule investigation and provisioning. Sprint planning my also trigger engineers to start their processes such as initiating data synchronization or virtual server copy.

The most important aspect of sprint planning is to start the conversation between application analysts and engineers who may not normally talk outside of a "ticketing" system. Communication between all technical resources as the application moves through the daily huddles and cut sheet reviews is critical and starts with sprint planning.

Slide 16 Daily Huddles

DAILY HUDDLES
15 minutes a day saves hours of frustration... or worse

App Analysts   Infra Engineers

15 minutes or less   Are you on track   Do you need help   Who can help   Follow up off line   Next

We have found the biggest bottle necks occur when requests go into email loops and it take days to resolve what a simple conversation could have taken care of in just a few minutes. The daily huddle askes each application analyst (that is in the sprint to the finish) if they are on track with the pre-move work and do they have any road blocks they need assistance to resolve. If there is a need, the right person to help is identified in the huddle and assigned to follow up right after.

Outside of the huddles, the project leaders are working with analysts and engineers on each cut sheet so there are few surprises in the huddle. The huddles usually highlight items such as "I didn't hear back on the firewall change yesterday, is that complete?" or "can the storage team confirm my data copy finished last night as expected?".

Occasionally an issue will come up that needs immediate announcement such as: "due to an extremely high census, the charge nurse just asked to postpone the move of xyz for one week.".   The analyst and project leader can now regroup afterward with the team to update communications, reschedule the move event and ensure the testers are aware of the new time without slowing down any final pre-move work. This way near real time adjustments can be made.

On average 15 to 25 applications may be in the daily huddle at any one time with representation from the infrastructure teams and other support groups. Issues, concerns, problems are raised in huddle and worked offline.

Slide 17 Iterative, Repeatable and Flexible

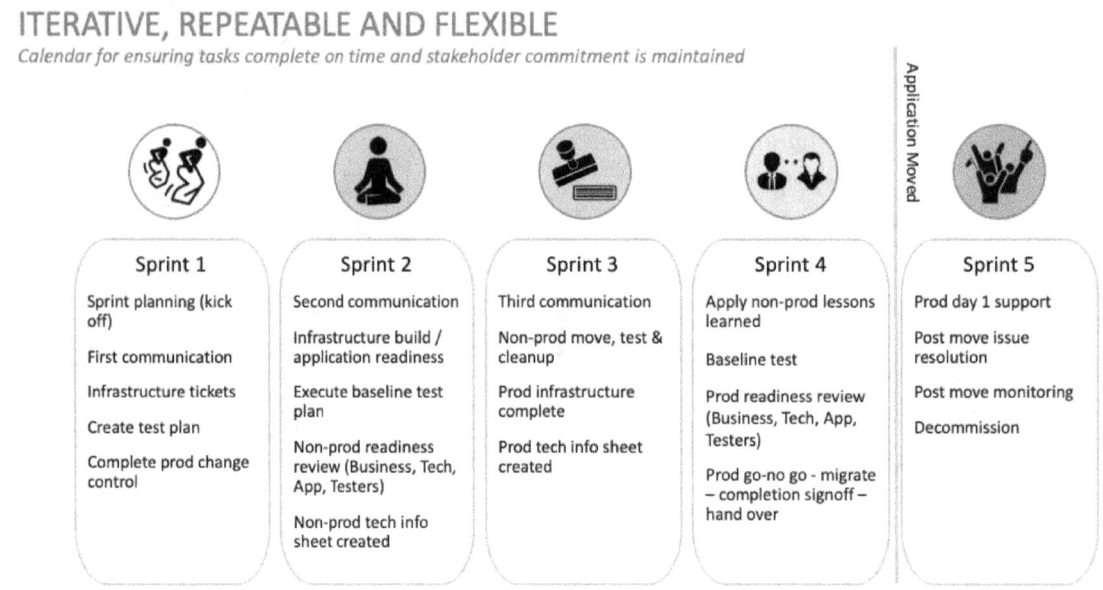

ITERATIVE, REPEATABLE AND FLEXIBLE
Calendar for ensuring tasks complete on time and stakeholder commitment is maintained

Sprint 1	Sprint 2	Sprint 3	Sprint 4	Sprint 5
Sprint planning (kick off)	Second communication	Third communication	Apply non-prod lessons learned	Prod day 1 support
First communication	Infrastructure build / application readiness	Non-prod move, test & cleanup	Baseline test	Post move issue resolution
Infrastructure tickets	Execute baseline test plan	Prod infrastructure complete	Prod readiness review (Business, Tech, App, Testers)	Post move monitoring
Create test plan	Non-prod readiness review (Business, Tech, App, Testers)	Prod tech info sheet created	Prod go-no go - migrate – completion signoff – hand over	Decommission
Complete prod change control	Non-prod tech info sheet created			

Slide 17 repeats some of the high-level actives that occur the weeks leading up to the move event. As you can see communication to the users occurs multiple times leading up to the event. One item to note is that it is best, if an application has a Dev / Test / QA system, that they be moved within the sprints before the production application. This allows lessons learned to be codified and applied progressively forward.

A word of caution: moving all applications' lower environments as a separate move event early in the schedule to test infrastructure may seem like a good idea but in reality, costs the project many valuable lessons at an application level to be lost. It is better to develop an infrastructure test plan that is independent of the applications.

It is critical to ensure an application baseline test is completed prior to the move so that baseline results can be compared to the post-move test results. Without a baseline test, final results can be misinterpreted. More than once, a tester has brought up a problem that after investigation and debugging, was determined to be the same behavior as before the move.

To declare the move event complete, all those involve give a "go" meaning the application, server, VIP, …. are working correctly or if an issue is found that is insignificant and it can be remediated later. An example of an insignificant issue is a printer needing to be rebooted when the remote office opens.

The first applications to go through the move train should be treated as pilot moves. Ten to 20 low risk applications selected by the application analysts and business owners should test out and refine your move train process as well as verify any uncertainty in the infrastructure or project assumptions.

Slide 18 High-Level Time-Line

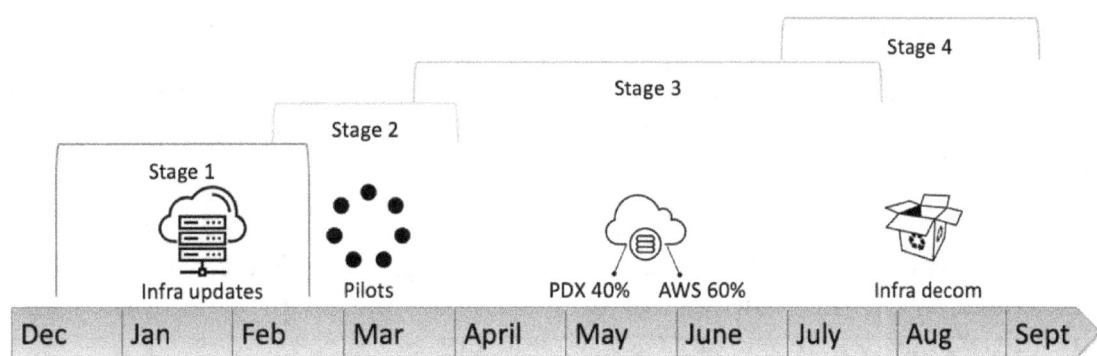

HIGH-LEVEL TIME-LINE
How soon do we have to get started and when are we done

High-level timing is important for everyone to understand. The duration of each stage should time-box the work at a high-level. In this example, stage 1's end is infrastructure's commitment to having the new datacenter ready to receive applications. Stage 2 and stage 3 put boundaries for analysts to negotiate their applications' move dates. Initially, general target dates within the boundaries are fine with details being finalized soon after.

The move matrix is the definitive schedule for each application. There is one row for every application (or service) and the rows should be in descending order according to production move date. An application has four stages:

- Back Log
- In Planning
- In Process
- Complete

Rather than a traditional Gantt chart schedule, the move matrix can be thought of as a Kanban. An application will start out as in back log. During this time the build sheet information should be completed and the concept of how the application will move worked out: V2V, build new, fork lift, ... About eight to twelve weeks prior to the move date, depending on complexity, the application's stage should change to "in planning" and the details of the cut sheet be fleshed out, vendors engaged, build sheets revalidated, test plans developed and final details confirmed.

When an application comes into sprint planning the stage shifts to in process and analysts attend daily huddles as well as hold multiple work sessions with engineers, testers and others to script cutover tasks and track pre-move progress. Two to three days prior to the move date, a go/no go review is held in which a step by step mock move is conducted to ensure all steps are accounted for and sequenced correctly. The final step in the review is to ensure a "go" from everyone involved.

Following the success of a move, the stage is changed to complete.

The move matrix itself has three sections. The top, or what we refer to as above the line are applications at the in-process stage. Just below the line are applications that are in planning followed by those in back log. The final section is "complete", where applications are moved to after their successful migration.

Since the move matrix is the definitive list of scope, all applications and services should have a row. In some cases, services may have a slightly different pattern for their move, but they should still complete all four stages and track through the move matrix for visibility.

Slide 19 What Now

WHAT NOW
How do I get ahead of the work and avoid a death march

Pick a Date	Complete Build Sheet	Complete Cut Sheet
Validate application state and destination	We'll fill in what we know to get you started	First pass, looking for 80%
Resolve competing priorities	Ask for help	Ask for help

Smart Sheet work space - https://app.smartsheet.com/...   19

This training package is typically reviewed early on with all the application analysts and engineers across multiple sessions. This may take several weeks to complete the rounds with all individuals. It is important to give individuals tasks to perform while the training continues with other groups. The major takeaway to complete for individuals is to collaborate with their customer on a date that will work best to move, which is why the initial high-level time line is a time box. Select a target date to move the application. This may initially be a particular month following a known black out period or major upgrade. For the accounting team, it might be following quarter end. 24x7 systems may pick a month and day of the week when they know they run the lowest usage. Regardless, the key is for analysts to engage with the business, discuss the information they have just received and work toward a date that fits into the rhythm of the business.

Slide 20 Wrap up

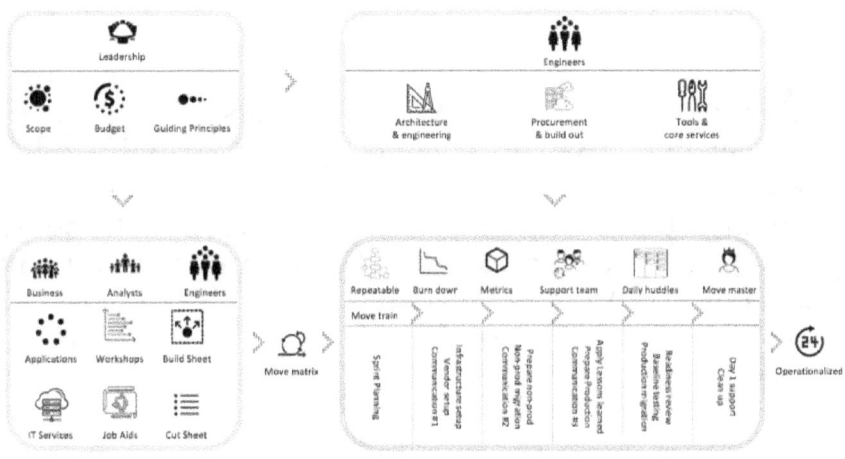

Slide 20 provides you an opportunity to bring your audience back to the overall concepts of the ROPE framework and how it's applied to your datacenter migration. Although everyone may not fully understand all the activities, they have a common baseline for your team to build on.

Slide 21 Important Links

IMPORTANT LINKS
Quick access to the tools, processes, and reporting

Dash Board	https://app.smartsheet.com/DC_Dashboard
Build Sheets	https://app.smartsheet.com/build sheet
Cut Sheets	https://app.smartsheet.com/cutsheet
RACI Matrix	https://www.dropbox.com/RACI
Application Migration Standard Approach	https://www.dropbox.com/migration_standard_approach
Training Presentation	https://www.dropbox.com/MicroMoveFrameworkTraining
Testing Presentation	https://www.dropbox.com/TestingTraining
Test Plan spreadsheet	https://www.dropbox.com/TestPlanTemplate
Status Reporting	https://www.dropbox.com/statusReports
Project Charter	https://www.dropbox.com/ProjectCharter
Communication Plan	https://www.dropbox.com/s/CommPlan
Executive Datacenter Migration Overview	https://www.dropbox.com/s/ExecutiveOverview

21

These links should be included in all the materials and status reports you share with stakeholders. By sharing and keeping the links in front of stakeholders you build a culture of self service and allow individuals to dive into the information they need most, when they need it. Of course you will have to update the links to correctly point to your documents in Smartsheet and other locations.

Slide 22 Q&A

What is the app move schedule?

What will my team have to do?

How can I help?

Who is deciding which apps go to the cloud?

How much time will this require from my staff?

22

If you don't have questions, it's an indication your audience hasn't been paying attention. You've given everyone a lot of information to digest in a short amount of time.

In the best case, you'll receive questions for edge cases you haven't considered. Acknowledge the value of the question and consider taking it into a collaborative session later so that together you can work through how this edge case may affect others. Just be sure to use the guiding principles, standard move document and the ROPE framework to stay within the boundaries of what you are trying to accomplish. When your project reaches its goal, everyone wins.

One last note is to start an FAQ document with the questions that come out of the training. You will be surprise how themes will develop around areas of concern and soon you will have answers that can be shared with everyone, demonstrating the team's ability to anticipate questions and have answers when needed.

Testing Training

Material Overview

No one will argue that the testing of an application move is paramount in order to validate success. Most people will also agree that testing a complex application can be difficult. One of the major advantages of "Like For Like" moves is the reduced amount and narrowed focus of the testing efforts. This chapter will review the test training deck under the assumption that a "Like for Like" move guiding principle is being followed and that the application's IP address, host name and VIPs will change, and applications will access IT services provided out of the new datacenter.

In cases where a build new or non-like for like method is being used to move an application, it is best to default to your organizations standard test methodology for an application upgrade or new release. In the case of a non-like for like migration, standard testing should include the unit testing and integration testing prior to the move (cutover) event. During the cutover (move event) of a build new or upgrade consider this training deck the minimum testing to perform. However, since a build new or component upgrade introduces a significant amount of change, the application analyst and business customer will need to determine the appropriate level of testing required at the cutover in order to sign off on the move.

If an existing test plan is available for an application from its implementation, upgrade, or DR failover, it should be used as a starting point.

An important consideration for testing is user / business customer involvement. There are multiple reasons to involve the customer in the testing during a move event. A few key reasons are:

- If your production system does not have test accounts and test scenarios built in, then you are testing using live data which is more of a validation than true test where you are attempting to break the system. Business users should be the only ones making changes to live production data.
- Business users who may normally ask you to move the application at 02:00 on Saturday, often decide the move event can take place on a week day after 16:30 if they are going to be required to be on the call and test.

Slide 1 Datacenter Migration Testing

DATACENTER
MIGRATION
TESTING

Keys To A Successful Approach
Leadership, Priority and Communication

The goal of this training deck is to discuss the base level testing required and the reasons for the test patterns we recommend.

Over the years we have found that an organization's QA group can and should play a vital role in testing during a datacenter move. If automated tests are owned by QA, then running those test cases during the move event is a natural extension of their current capabilities. However, most of the organizations we have worked with have a very small footprint covered by automated testing. If they have automated testing it is limited to small portions of a few in-house developed applications.

The norm for application testing at many past clients has been to rely on analysts to install and test COTS (commercial off the shelf) applications with very little QA involvement. This situation is made more difficult when application responsibilities have been passed around as analysts have left the company and there is little or no testing documentation. In many cases the datacenter move may be the first time the analyst has really had to dig into the application.

Couple the lack of consistent COTS testing methodology with the number and pace of moves, and it becomes clear the role of QA needs to shift. Rather than expecting QA to write and preform the tests themselves, QA becomes the coach and coordinator of testing executed by the application analysts and business users.

 In the role of coach and coordinator, QA is more than a report generator. QA brings consistency using standard testing templates, review of tests plans and actively running the test effort during the move event. The tasks for QA are to reinforce the value of testing what has changed, provide support to analysts by coaching on the test plan creation and ensure the auditability of testing. The responsibility of testing and sign-off remains with the application analysts and business owners who must sign off with a "go" during the move event.

If your organization does not have the QA function, a standard level of testing will need to be agreed to. Additionally, resources must be accounted for to fill the QA function as discussed above. In the past, this effort has been approximately one to two full time resources spread across a number of individuals to staff each of the moves. Ideally your lead QA member will present this test training.

Slide 2 Tools That Work

TOOLS THAT WORK
Focus work and effort where it will deliver the best results

Build Sheet	Cut Sheet	Test Spreadsheet
Reuse the build sheet	Attach your test plan to the cut sheet	Spread sheet with test scenarios
List of Interfaces for interface testing already defined	Baseline Test	Pre-populated template
	Post move Test	Application and interface tests
	Back-out plan Test	

Slide 2 starts by discussing how the tools discussed prior in the move training support testing. The starting point is the build sheet. As mentioned previously one of the more difficult items to document is the application's interfaces. That hard work now pays dividends by providing the outline for test cases. In a "Like For Like" move, the application's functionality remains the same and should not require testing. This avoids having to develop and execute long, complex test plans designed to check the accuracy of business rules and functional behavior. Instead, the change, and therefore the test cases, are limited to the interfaces in and out of the application. Analyst can be assured test coverage by writing a test case for each interface documented in the build sheet.

The cut sheet assists analysts with timing their test work. There should be a task for creating the test plan and executing that plan as a baseline prior to the move event. A baseline test is the execution of the test plan on the application and interfaces in the current datacenter prior to the move event producing documented results.

The baseline test serves several purposes. First, the baseline validates the tests can be run as expected and measures how long testing efforts will require during the move event. It may also highlight where transactions need to be held up to ensure records are available for post move testing of the workflow. The second point is it produces the expected results or current behavior to validate against during the move event testing.

More than once on a move event, analysts or business users have called out a test as failed forcing a rollback only to find out later the test result was correct, but a lack of baseline results prevented a quick verification of how the application behaves versus desired or imagined results. In a "Like For Like" move, if a function is broken prior the move event, it will remain broken after the move event.

The test plan may need to be slightly tweaked for a roll back. For example, if a test case calls out a new FQDN (fully qualified domain name) to use in order to reach the application, the old FQDN will need to be substituted.

In order to maintain consistency, QA will want to create a simple template (spread sheet or Smartsheet) that analysts can build on. The template usually has some basic smoke tests cases:

- RDP to server validate log-in at server level
- Log-in to application validate identity management
- Simple case to validate database connectivity

The remainder of the simple testing template allows the analyst to put in the required information in order to ensure the interface interactions are validated.

At this point bring up the template to show the audience the testing template they will be filling out for each application.

While an application is moved once, it may be required to be test multiple times. The application is tested for its move as well as when any of its interfaces move.

Slide 3 Field Of Play In A Move

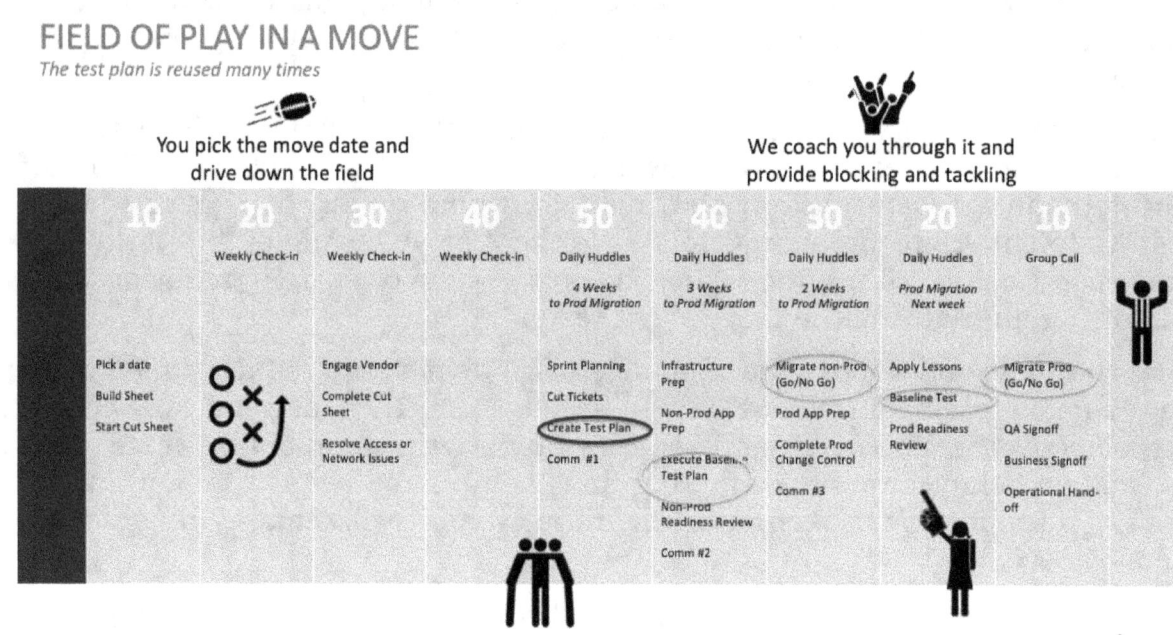

Using the field of play slide again from the framework deck, analysts can see where testing activities fit into the process. Because the testing is limited to interfaces, the duration of these tasks should not require more than a few hours each.

Slide 4 Non-interfacing Vendor Applications

WHAT AND WHEN DO I NEED TO TEST
Non-interfacing vendor applications

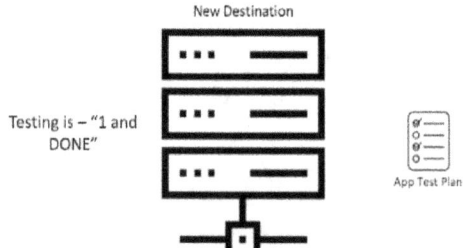

Non-interfacing (stand-alone) vendor applications
These are vendor application that (in most cases) will be installed production ready and testing or verification will take place in the "production" environment.

Validation steps:
- Software is installed, configured, validated and accessible to testers
- Software acceptance tested for sign-off

Slide 4 describes the simplest case, a standalone server managed by a vendor. No interfaces, no interactions with other devices. The fact that the application is vendor owned or managed is called out since many times production is the only environment and the vendor may be the only one with credentials to the server in order to validate log files for errors on startup. Additionally, the vendor should participate in the move and be prepared to remediate issues if the testers are unable to log in or execute the basic tests.

Users simply login, perform work and log out. The test cases for this move are considered a smoke test. If the customer can log in and pull up a couple of screens to ensure data access, the move was successful.

Slide 5 Non-interfacing Applications Standalone

WHAT AND WHEN DO I NEED TO TEST
Non-interfacing applications stand alone

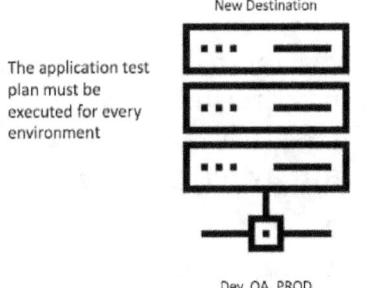

New Destination

The application test plan must be executed for every environment

App Test Plan

Dev, QA, PROD

Non-interfacing (stand-alone) applications
Testing teams should create a re-usable application test plan that can be applied to every environment. This test plan should have test results documented per environment (Dev, QA, Prod)

Validation steps:
• Software is installed, configured, validated and accessible to testers
• Software acceptance tested for sign-off

Like the non-interfacing vendor application above, slide 5 discusses a standalone server. The primary difference is in this version the standalone application has internal staff responsible for creating and executing the tests as well as checking the log files for errors on startup. In the case of multiple environments, the test plan will be reused as the moves progress through the environments.

Slide 6 Interfacing Point To Point Applications For Build New

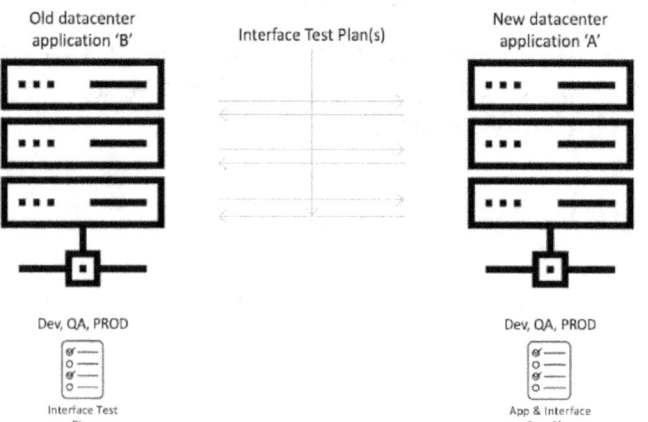

WHAT AND WHEN DO I NEED TO TEST
Interfacing point to point applications for build new

Old datacenter application 'B'

Interface Test Plan(s)

New datacenter application 'A'

Dev, QA, PROD

Interface Test Plan

Dev, QA, PROD

App & Interface Test Plan

Interfacing (Point to Point) Applications

These are applications that interface with other systems through a point to point connection, FTP or file shares. Not through the enterprise service bus.

Verification steps for all environments:

- Software and related components are installed, configured, validated and accessible to testers
- Software acceptance tested for sign-off
- Interfaces are tested for sign-off

In slide 6, the discussion turns to building a new version of the application and testing it prior to cut over. Like before when testing interfaces, be sure to test both directions in the case of bi-directional interfaces. It may be necessary to "hold" files or records in order to ensure there is data available to test the interface.

In a build new move, the analyst will need to perform full functional tests prior to the move (cut over). These pre-move tests will need to follow the same test methods used by your organization for any application upgrade. In the case of a data migration requirement, the pre-move should also validate data integrity. During the move event record counts should be validated to ensure data consistency between systems. The move event will also validate the interface as they change to point to/from the new datacenter version of the application interfaces. The interface testing should also include load balancing and other IT services.

Slide 7 V2V Or Interface Testing; When Something You Connect To Moves

WHAT AND WHEN DO I NEED TO TEST

V2V or interface testing: when something you connect to moves, test it

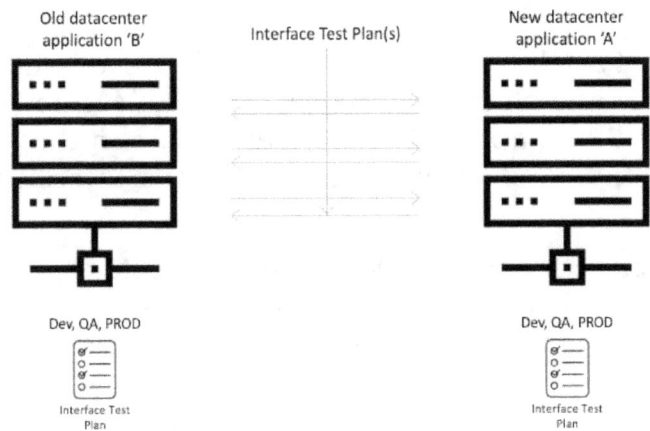

Slide 7 reiterates the fact that in the micro move framework, applications may have to test their interfaces multiple times over the course of the project. Although V2V move implies a virtual server move, the above case also holds true for physical moves. In this example, testers for applications "A" and "B" will be required to test interfaces when "A" moves and again when "B" moves.

The simple case used in this slide with server "A" and "B" will often bring up the question: "why not move 'A' and 'B' together which would only require testing once?" It is true in this simple case where two applications only talk to each other, it may reduce the testing effort, but by combining moves for testing reasons, you start to over optimize items that are not necessarily the bottle neck. Application "B" may consist of dozens of servers. Application "B" which is not moving in this case, may also communicate with dozens of other applications which will be tested when "B" moves. Applications "A" and "B" may be simple, yet critical business applications owned by different groups who cannot take downtime in the same window.

There are a host of reasons that may prevent application "A" and "B" moving together. The focus needs to be on moving applications within the rhythm of the business and only adding the complexity of moving groups of applications where it is absolutely necessary.

Any analysts who are responsible for the organization's interface engine can expect to be on dozens of or even hundreds of move events to perform testing. They are often required to turn down and back up interfaces as part of the move event to prevent data loss or transmission errors.

Testing conclusion

As we have repeatedly stated, small manageable "Like For Like" application migrations can move through the process more quickly than large complex move groups. This fact is demonstrated in the testing of applications as they move. Testing should ensure changes are accounted for and operating correctly. Testing the interface locations provides the full coverage to validate a successful move.

There will be cases when groups of applications may have to be moved and tested together such as in the case of a shared database. The test window may have to increase to allow time for all the applications to participate in the test, but the tests themselves should still focus on the connections and interfaces that have changed.

For applications that are not a "Like For Like" move, additional tests cases will need to be created in order to cover all changes beyond the interfaces. QA should coach analysts in documenting and testing all the changes that will occur with the move event.

The testing approach laid out in this slide deck represents our experience of moving applications using different methods. Typically, project management cannot dictate testing requirements. Therefore, the ROPE framework aligns responsibility to those most capable of completing the task. The information above provides guidance and recommendations, but the application analyst and business customer own the accountability for signing off the move event. They must create and execute tests that allow them to feel comfortable giving a "go". This approach follows the guiding principle of "App Teams Got This - App analysts own the migration, infrastructure teams support them throughout the migration".

Stakeholder Communication

The ROPE framework considers consistent, clear, timely communication vital to the success of any complex technology project. We have found that a project will receive tremendous support from the user community when they know what is happening. It will also receive criticism, even if everything goes smoothly, when there are surprises.

Clear communication to stakeholders is extremely important and one of the easiest items to maintain when planned for appropriately. A central theme for communications is to follow the old adage, tell what you want to tell them, tell them, tell them what you told them. Three communications for each application being moved has proven to be effective over the years.

Because communication is so important the following will provide guidance around what a job aid for application move communication might look like.

Example communication job aid

One of the guiding principles most senior leaders will agree on is:

Involve Me

Stakeholders actively engaged and awareness is apparent

In order to follow senior leadership's guidance, we typically established a clear, consistent method for communication to stakeholders affected by an application or IT service move. This job aid example lays out how to execute the datacenter migration project stakeholder communication for an application move event. You are encouraged to pull in the corporate communication team, service desk and other communication experts within your organization to develop your communication templates. Involving these groups in the development steps will ensure their continued support of the project throughout the entire process.

In addition to following a common communication process, analysts are encouraged to work directly with key stakeholders and follow any communication processes established for their individual application.

For each application move (or application component if one application is broken up into several moves) sending out three (3) stakeholder communications is recommended. Allowing stakeholders three opportunities to review the communication ensures busy individuals don't lose track of important project dates and times affecting their workflow.

To maintain a clear, consistent message to all the stakeholders, and follow the "Keep It Repeatable" guiding principle, a standard email template should be used to craft application move communication to stakeholders.

Step 1: Determine communication schedule

The timing of the communication is three (3) weeks before, two (2) weeks before and one (1) week before the application move date. Once an analyst has worked with their business partner to determine the appropriate move date and time, the schedule for sending out communication can be set.

Sunday	Monday	Tuesday	Wednesday	Thursday	Friday	Saturday
1	2	3	4	5 Send email #1	6	7
8	9	10	11	12 Send email #2	13	14
15	16	17	18	19 Send email #3	20	21
22	23	24	25	26 Move date	27	28
29	30	31				

To assist with the communication schedule, after the analyst enters the move date into the cut sheet, the cut sheet can calculate recommended communication dates. You may need to adjust these dates, but they should provide a solid guideline.

Step 2: Identify the stakeholders

Every application is different. Some application moves may only affect two or three users and their manager. Other applications such as EDI (enterprise data interchange) may affect the entire enterprise. It is important to consider whose work flow or support team may be affected by the application move. In the EDI example, other applications that use EDI to exchange information may have their files wait in the queue while the move occurs. These stakeholders should also be informed. Review the build sheet and consider all the application interfaces when considering stakeholder identification.

Once the stakeholders have been identified, create a list of email addresses required to reach all of the stakeholders. This may be individual names or a team distribution-list. Work with the business owner to ensure complete coverage. You may want to divide the list between "TO:" stakeholders and "CC: stakeholders.

Tip: Include yourself on the cc list. The standard temple's cc list should already include support groups, managers and others who have requested to be on all application move notifications.

Step 3: Craft the communication

All stakeholder move notifications should use the standard move communication template. The template is an outlook email template and will allow you to quickly develop your stakeholder message. By standardizing the communications, you ensure stakeholders receive the required information and everyone quickly recognizes the impact.

Download and open the <<put link in here to a template>>. The template will open in Outlook as an email message with the following:

Datacenter Migration Change Notification (P-Code IUS23138) <<Application Name>>	
What:	As a part of the <<location>> facility closure the <<Application Name>> is being moved out of the <<location>> datacenter.
When:	Date: <<mmm dd, yyyy>>
Change Window:	Start time: <<hh:mm am/pm – time zone>> End time: <<hh:mm am/pm – time zone>>
How does this affect you:	<<explain which users or user groups are affected by the outage and any items they need to be aware of during the event window. For example: "Western region Kronos will be unavailable for all users located in CA, OR, and Alaska. During the down time follow your business unit's manual recording process for time entry">>
For more information contact:	<<Application analyst name>>

All placeholders within brackets << >> should be replaced with the appropriate information.

Begin by inserting the application's name in the email's subject line, at the top of the message and on the "What:" line.

On the "When:" line, enter the date of the move. Please spell out the month and use a four-digit year. For example: March 13, 2017.

On the "Change Window:" line, enter the start and end times for the move. This time should match the time submitted and approved in the change control. Since stakeholders may be located across the globe, include the time zone and an am/pm designation for both the start and end time.

The "How does this affect you:" is critical to ensuring stakeholders know how the move will affect them. Be clear but brief. It may be as simple as the XXX application will be unavailable during the move window. If there are business continuity activities that should be used during the move window they should be called out in this section of the communication. Applications that interface with your application should be called out and how they will be affected. For example: All applications using EDI will continue to work but their file transfers will be delayed until the move is complete. This information is for the business stakeholders and should not be technical.

Finally, include your name and possibly the business owner's name in case stakeholders have additional questions or concerns about the application move.

Once the message is complete, fill in the TO: and CC: lines with the stakeholder emails you previously identified.

In your Outlook client, select "Save As" in order to save your communication to your desktop. Use the "Save As Type" of "Outlook Template" with the name "<<application name>> <<location>> Datacenter Migration Change Notification".

Step 4: Getting it out to the stakeholders

For many of our clients, communication is sent out from one location. In some cases, this was an automated tool in other cases the NOC or change control team sent out the communications. These groups normally have the ability to send messages to distribution groups that the average analyst cannot.

We recommend these communications go out via a central mailbox to enhance consistency and ensure delivery. The steps needed to ensure central distribution should be documented. For example:

Following this process allows the change control team to send out your stakeholder notifications for you on the schedule you set. By having change control send out communications, stakeholders can be ensured the move is following appropriate change policy.

In order to have the change control team send out your stakeholder notification, you will attach your "<<application name>> <<location>> Datacenter Migration Change Notification" (email template file) and "<<application name>> change notification schedule" (text or word file) to your change control. This means you will need to start your change control early enough to ensure your communication is available to the change control team so that they can send them out following your schedule.

Beyond email

Communication is about conveying an idea or message to others in a way they can easily consume and will understand. Email is a delivery system, not the communication. What you deliver through email or other media needs to speak in your audience's vernacular, be easily consumable, and convey meaningful information to them when they receive it in a timely manner.

Throughout a datacenter migration there will be many times complex technical messages must be shared with stakeholders and team members. The rule we use is simple: use imagery to convey the message's meaning, words should be minimal. If the message is in text format, the complete idea should be conveyed in 100 words or less.

This simple rule is harder than it sounds. Communicating a complex technical message with brevity and accuracy requires you to consolidate your thoughts and become crystal clear on your message as well as the action you want to drive.

For example: During a datacenter migration project, engineers working on another project outside the datacenter migration project implemented a change that caused several critical applications to crash in the old datacenter. This change sent the business into a panic, demanding that network changes pause for 90 days. Across the enterprise rumors ran rampant about what that meant to the datacenter migration project. Engineers and application analysts felt the safe path was to put their application or service moves on hold. The project management team knew there were alternatives in order to stay on plan.

The first thing needed was to understand why there was so much vibration and concern. This client's IT organization had struggled with changes causing major unplanned outages and in the past the culture affixed blame as well as quickly stopped all change work to pacify angry customers. While the culture was changing to be more root cause focused, communication of remediation plans and next steps were not always shared with everyone, leaving word of mouth as the primary means of communication. The datacenter move project was caught in the middle of the rumors with many different versions stating how the outage would affect scheduled application moves.

In order to bring business users, application analyst, engineer and leadership all onto the same page a simple decision tree was developed that allowed anyone to answer the question "Can I move it?".

Can I move it decision tree

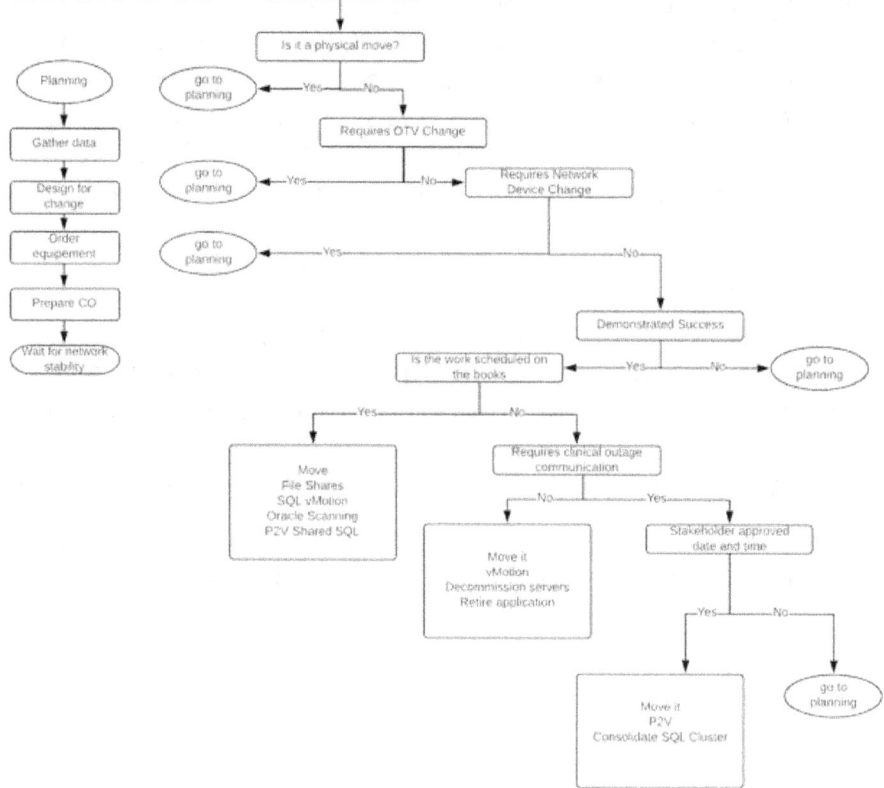

Approved by senior leadership to guide continuing progress while the network stabilizes.

Using the datacenter move project's existing meetings and communication plan, the decision tree was first socialized with business and technical leadership to ensure they agreed and would amplify the message with their staff. Then the decision tree was covered in the daily huddle with all the individuals who had applications on the move train. Next it was shared at the weekly managers meeting and individual team check-ins. Finally, a copy was added to the project status report and posted to the project dashboard, visible to all.

Having this one simple slide and sharing it through conversations with the stakeholders we easily put to rest fears individuals had about getting in trouble for going against a freeze request. The decision tree removed their uncertainty and allowed the team to shift the few affected applications into a short re-planning exercise while the majority continued the course. The datacenter migration project maintained its momentum.

This example is not unusual with complex projects that span large enterprises. As the datacenter migration project's management team, it is your responsibility to continually assess the communication need, get crystal clear on the message and then determine the best way to convey that message using language and imagery your stakeholders will quickly grasp.

The ROPE framework has several planned communication and reporting methods designed to maintain transparency but there is always an ongoing need for the project's leadership team to respond to risks, issues and concerns with targeted messages.

Visualization

A very powerful way to communicate critical information is through the visualization of metrics. You can see this power demonstrated by the wide spread marketing use of infographics. The specific metrics conveyed through visualization depends on the stage of the datacenter migration and information needing to be communicated.

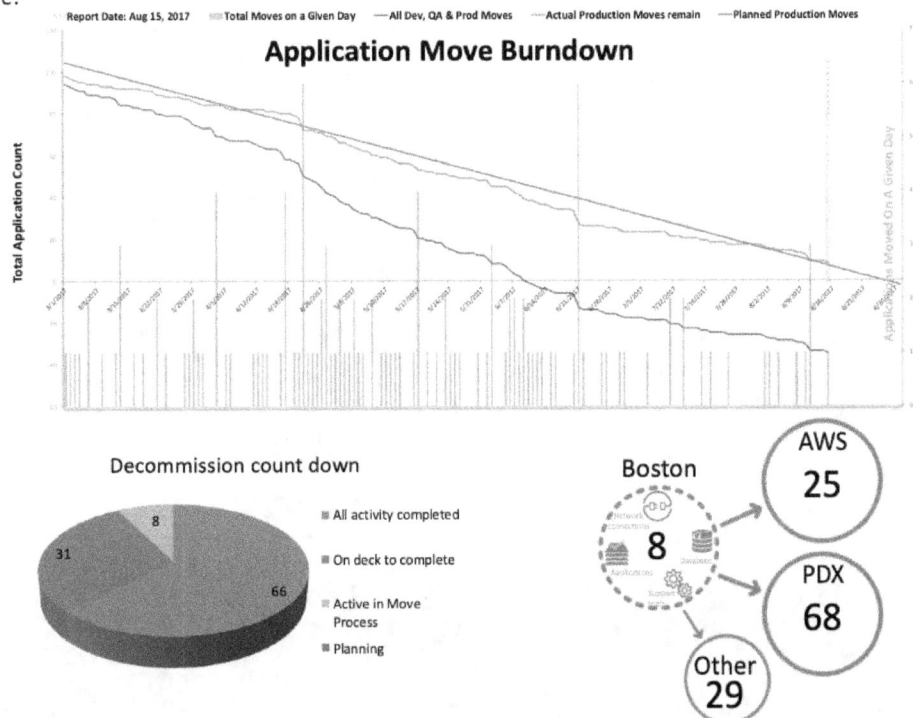

Program metrics at a glance
Purpose: Simple yet powerful metrics that provide the health of program's activities at a glance.

Humans are visual creatures. A large percentage of our brain is dedicated to the visual process. Our love of images lies deep within our cognitive ability to pay attention. Images grab people's attention easily and draws us in.

Humans process images at an alarming speed, 6,000 times faster than text. When we see a picture, we analyze it within a very short snippet of time, understanding the meaning and impact within.

Project text data, even important metrics, don't always come across as personal to individuals. People may not feel concern about a certain metric or risk because they are not emotionally invested in it. This isn't because stakeholders are unconcerned. It's because sometimes these metrics just aren't reaching out in the way they ought to.

Images help us become involved. With images, we see the project and its goals. The images contribute to the storytelling process that can make the datacenter migration project more engaging. This is what makes infographics so popular: they crunch down data and findings and present them in an easy to digest manner.

Both of the following convey the same information, how many applications have been moved where. The text requires additional effort to read each line, digest it, then reassemble it back into the larger meaning it is conveying while the image puts it all together for the viewer to be quickly absorbed.

"We have moved 68 applications to Portland, 25 applications have moved to AWS and 29 applications have moved to other locations.   Eight applications remain in Boston and are schedule to move."

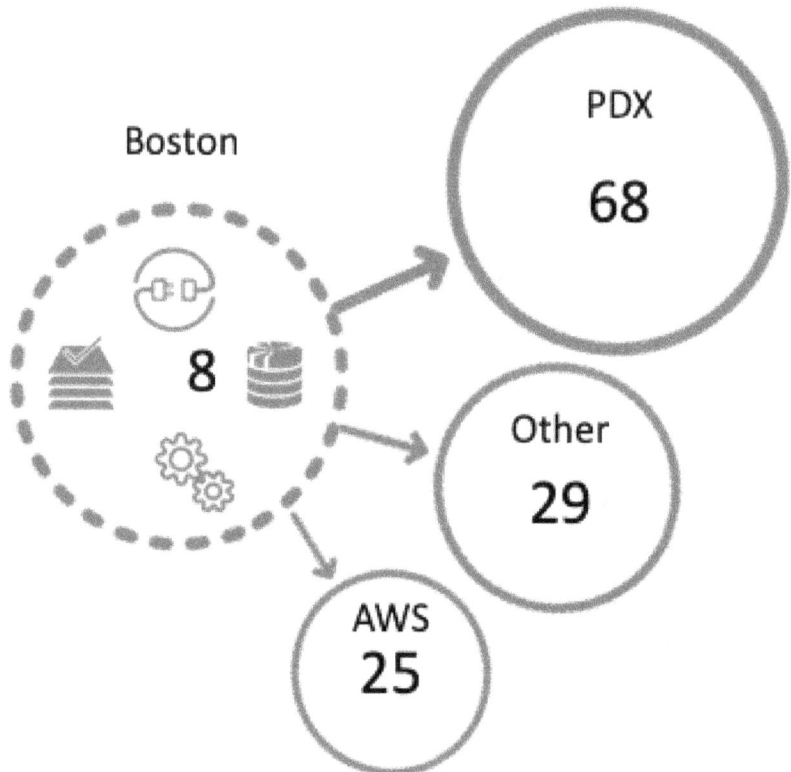

As you will see in the dashboard discussion below, a burn up or burn down chart can be a very powerful method for conveying overall project progress and health. Rather than provide specific individual move stats, the burn down provides a clear indicator as to the project's actual velocity compared to the planned velocity.

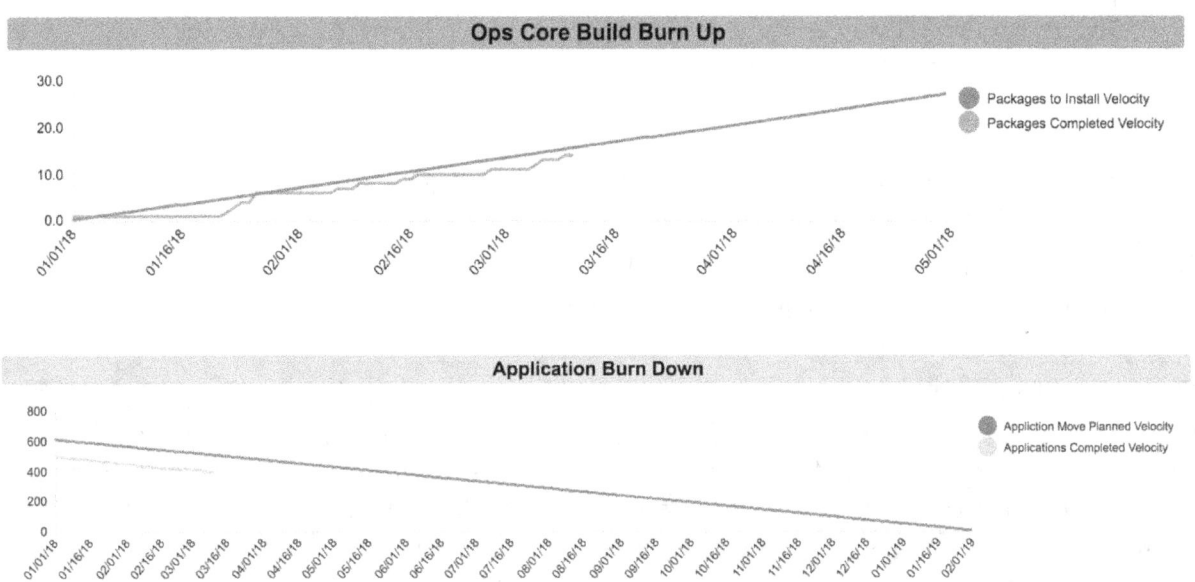

We suggest using the burn down and burn up graphs to communicate trend and elevate visibility to points of concerns. In other words, if the actual velocity is trending along the planned velocity and the project team can explain short variances off of the planned velocity the project is on track.

A burn up or burn down will allow any stakeholder to quickly grasp the health of the datacenter migration project, if they know how to read it. Individuals who are used to seeing Gantt charts, with tasks arbitrarily assigned a percentage complete, may require some coaching in order to shift their thinking in sequential terms. The value of the burn down or burn up is in its ability to quickly convey progress and initiate conversations around that progress.

Images are a vital part of datacenter migration communication and should be included over long blocks of text. In order to break down the complex messages of datacenter migrations, you need the help of visuals.

Dashboard and Status

Every organization has a preferred project status reporting format. When we work for a client, we adopt their status format and timing guidelines in order to provide information in a way the client is used to consuming it from projects.

The key to status reporting is brevity. The less words used to convey the same status information, the more powerful the message becomes. Readers have a tremendous amount of material to get through on any given day, they appreciate project teams who respect their time by distilling status information into concise focused updates.

The project status report should be reviewed with stakeholders and represent the opening topic of the following meetings:

- Weekly project owner's weekly review.

- Steering board.
- Management guidance team
- Weekly managers meeting.

The status report should also be distributed via email to stakeholders involved on a weekly basis.

Status reporting it is a staple of project management and an important part of any complex project. However, we believe this is the first step in communicating progress.

Following the ROPE framework, our datacenter migration dashboard[6] provides a central location for all project information. It delivers different levels of information required by different stakeholders in an easily consumable format. Executives can quickly visualize the datacenter migration's progress as well as review the major risks in order to focus their attention. Individual department managers can see what activities are in process and how their teams are performing. The project management office can evaluate the datacenter migration project to ensure it is meeting their standards and passing all quality gates.

The following is an example of a datacenter migration dashboard. This dashboard reflected a project in the final stages of the DR datacenter build while in parallel preparing and moving the first batch of pilot move applications into its new primary datacenter.

---

[6] You can use many different tools to build a dashboard, we use Smartsheet.

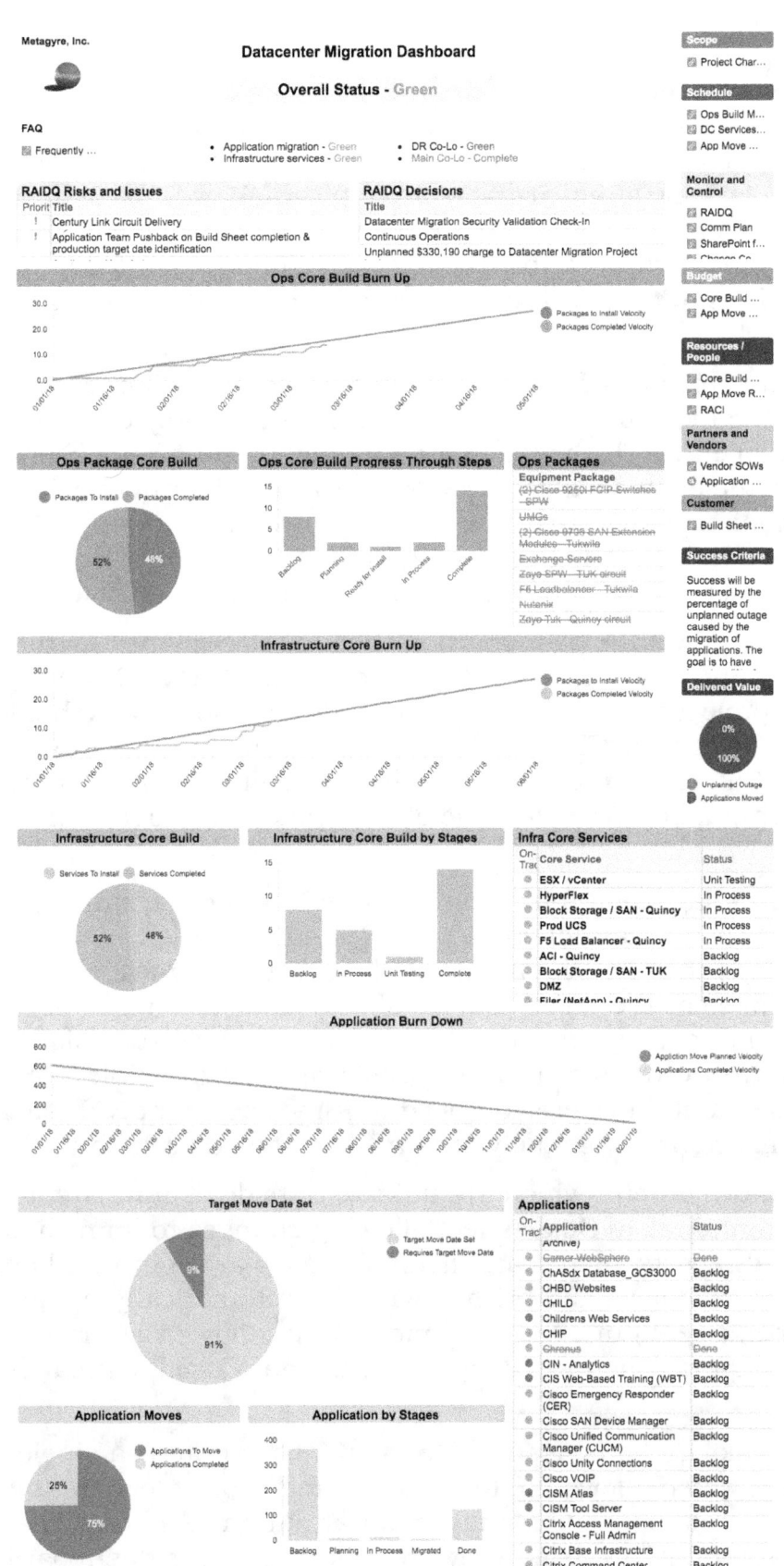

Metagyre, Inc.

Datacenter Migration Dashboard

Overall Status - Green

FAQ

☑ Frequently ...
- Application migration - Green
- Infrastructure services - Green
- DR Co-Lo - Green
- Main Co-Lo - Complete

RAIDQ Risks and Issues

Priorit	Title
!	Century Link Circuit Delivery
!	Application Team Pushback on Build Sheet completion & production target date identification

RAIDQ Decisions

Title

Datacenter Migration Security Validation Check-In

Continuous Operations

Unplanned $330,190 charge to Datacenter Migration Project

Scope
- ☑ Project Char...

Schedule
- ☑ Ops Build M...
- ☑ DC Services...
- ☑ App Move ...

Monitor and Control
- ☑ RAIDQ
- ☑ Comm Plan
- ☑ SharePoint f...
- ☑ Change Co...

Budget
- ☑ Core Build ...
- ☑ App Move ...

Resources / People
- ☑ Core Build ...
- ☑ App Move R...
- ☑ RACI

Partners and Vendors
- ☑ Vendor SOWs
- ⊙ Application ...

Customer
- ☑ Build Sheet ...

Success Criteria

Success will be measured by the percentage of unplanned outage caused by the migration of applications. The goal is to have

Ops Core Build Burn Up

- Packages to Install Velocity
- Packages Completed Velocity

Ops Package Core Build

- Packages To Install
- Packages Completed
- 52% / 48%

Ops Core Build Progress Through Steps

Backlog, Planning, Ready for Install, In Process, Complete

Ops Packages

Equipment Package
(2) Cisco 9250i FCIP Switches - SPW
UMGs
(2) Cisco 9706 SAN Extension Modules - Tukwila
Exchange Servers
Zayo SPW - TUK circuit
F5 Loadbalancer - Tukwila
Nutanix
Zayo Tuk - Quincy circuit

Infrastructure Core Burn Up

- Packages to Install Velocity
- Packages Completed Velocity

Delivered Value

0% / 100%

- Unplanned Outage
- Applications Moved

Infrastructure Core Build

- Services To Install
- Services Completed
- 52% / 48%

Infrastructure Core Build by Stages

Backlog, In Process, Unit Testing, Complete

Infra Core Services

On-Track	Core Service	Status
⊙	ESX / vCenter	Unit Testing
⊙	HyperFlex	In Process
⊙	Block Storage / SAN - Quincy	In Process
⊙	Prod UCS	In Process
⊙	F5 Load Balancer - Quincy	In Process
⊙	ACI - Quincy	Backlog
⊙	Block Storage / SAN - TUK	Backlog
⊙	DMZ	Backlog
⊙	Filer (NetApp) - Quincy	Backlog

Application Burn Down

- Application Move Planned Velocity
- Applications Completed Velocity

Target Move Date Set

- Target Move Date Set
- Requires Target Move Date
- 9% / 91%

Applications

On-Track	Application	Status
	Archive)	
⊙	Cerner WebSphere	Done
⊙	ChASdx Database_GCS3000	Backlog
⊙	CHBD Websites	Backlog
⊙	CHILD	Backlog
⊙	Childrens Web Services	Backlog
⊙	CHIP	Backlog
⊙	Chronus	Done
⊙	CIN - Analytics	Backlog
⊙	CIS Web-Based Training (WBT)	Backlog
⊙	Cisco Emergency Responder (CER)	Backlog
⊙	Cisco SAN Device Manager	Backlog
⊙	Cisco Unified Communication Manager (CUCM)	Backlog
⊙	Cisco Unity Connections	Backlog
⊙	Cisco VOIP	Backlog
⊙	CISM Atlas	Backlog
⊙	CISM Tool Server	Backlog
⊙	Citrix Access Management Console - Full Admin	Backlog
⊙	Citrix Base Infrastructure	Backlog
⊙	Citrix Command Center	Backlog

Application Moves

- Applications To Move
- Applications Completed
- 25% / 75%

Application by Stages

Backlog, Planning, In Process, Migrated, Done

Breaking down the dashboard there are two types of information: static and real-time. The majority of static content runs along the right side of the dashboard as links placed under headers matching the PMO's breakdown of project artifacts. The static artifacts are typically Word, Excel or Power Point documents stored in the project's SharePoint, Dropbox or Wiki. These project artifacts are generally prescribed by the PMO and are developed using their templates. Links to these artifacts are provided in order to ensure quick central access.

Static artifacts typically called out on the dashboard included: project charter, budget tracking tool, communication plan and other project management office required documents. The artifacts are grouped based on the client's PMO standard. In the example above the PMO grouped their documents by Scope, Schedule, Monitor and Control, Budget, Resources, Vendor and Customer. The dashboard reflected their grouping in order to provide consistency with other projects across the enterprise and maintain familiarity for stakeholders.

A link that we add on the dashboard is the FAQ document. As the project starts out, a trend of questions begins to develop. The FAQ provides the answers the project wants to circulate in order to inform stakeholders and reduce misinformation. The FAQ is a living document. It can be developed in Word, Excel, Smartsheet or another familiar medium. The document should be maintained throughout the life cycle of the datacenter migration project as questions evolve.

Most project management offices have a standard for marking a project "Green – on track", "Yellow – has concerns", or "Red – in trouble". We recommend you follow that standard. This is the first indicator a visitor will see and should immediately present the overall status of the datacenter migration project. We also recommend making the individual workstreams status color visible. Making both the overall status and workstream status visible, you can focus stakeholders' attention where you need it. Since some individuals are color blind, it is important to use the word and color together such as GREEN.

Unlike the static content, which are links to outside documents, the dynamic content is maintained in Smartsheet allowing changes to immediately reflect on the dashboard reports, charts and lists. As tasks are completed and checked off the dashboard charts and burn downs are automatically updated. In addition to being real time, the dynamic content allows viewers to click on a widget or chart and drill down deeper into the data used to create the dashboard.

The RAIDq (Risks, Actions, Issues, Decisions, Question) is a single sheet kept in Smartsheet which allows the tower leads and project leaders to record and track project items requiring management attention. As items change disposition in the RAIDq sheet, they are reflected on the dashboard's two reports. We have found that it is important to highlight both risks and decision on the dashboard in order to drive required action and communicate course corrections. Clicking on either of the dashboard's RAIDq reports will bring the viewer into the RAIDq sheet allowing them to investigate the details.

The dynamic content for each workstream is color coded in order to provide a visual grouping. Each grouping contains a burn down or burn up, a chart showing over all velocity trend against the plan. The delivered velocity being plotted depends on the grouping. For example: the physical build out might track completed cabinets or individual pieces of equipment depending on the size of the build. The infrastructure core build typically tracks the key infrastructure services required to open the datacenter such as DMZ, block storage replication or core routing and switching. For the application burn down, each application and individual service is represented as a deliverable in the planned velocity.

Along with the burn down chart a simple pie or donut chart shows completed and remaining deliverables along with a chart showing status of each item is (back log, in process, testing, completed, ...). Like a Kanban board these charts allow everyone to see work in progress and where any big flow problems may exist.

The last required report for each grouping is a simple list of the deliverable items being tracked and their status. Clicking on the list will bring up that groups move matrix allowing full details of each item to be revealed for further investigation.

Additional charts and indicators can be added as needed throughout the project to highlight items needing attention. In the case of the application groupings, application analysts were having difficulty setting target move dates. A chart was added to visualize what percentage of applications had not yet set a target move date. When the chart was initially added to the dashboard, 85% of the application owners had not set a target move date. Within two weeks of reporting, that percentage dropped to below 10% and the majority of those remaining 10% had committed to set target start dates within an acceptable time frame. The power of visualizing a metric and providing a desired action for changing that metric cannot be over stated.

A link to the dashboard should be included in all communication to stakeholders. When questions come up from stakeholders, reference where they can find the information on the dashboard and walk them through the process of finding it. If you can continually demonstrate the dashboard's value to stakeholders you will find it becomes a valuable, self-service, one stop location for datacenter migration project information.

Below is the base level datacenter move dashboard. This is the initial dashboard deployed at the beginning of the project along with required sheets to drive the dashboard.

NewCo Datacenter Program

Scope Change
70%
30%
○ Original Scope ○ Added Scope

Move Status
6
1
○ On track ○ Concerns

Budget / Spend
$10,750
$600
○ Spent ○ Remaining Budget

FAQ

Scope

Project Charter

Schedule

Build Out Matr...
Move Matrix - ...

Monitoring

RAIDa Log - ...
Communicatio...
Proj Change ...
Proj Document

Budget

Budget - New...

Resources / People

RACI - NewC...

Partners and Vendors

Vendor SOWs

Customer

Build Sheet M...

Key Contacts
Mark Hinkelman
Marc Swenson
Karen Grose
Tim Adamsen
Beverly Baker-b

Provide Feedback

Quick Status
Scope   - ○
Schedule - ○
Status   - ○

Headline News
Lorem ipsum dolor sit amet, consectetur adipiscing elit, sed do eiusmod tempor incididunt ut labore et dolore magna aliqua. Ut enim ad minim veniam, quis nostrud exercitation ullamco laboris nisi ut aliquip ex ea commodo consequat.

RAIDa Log - Open Items

RAIDC Priority	Title	Plan
Risk	Application Knowledge	Will develop build sheets and run scan tool
Risk	Competing Priorities	Train staff on required involvement and work. Escalate as appropriate. Have completed training for identified groups as of 2/20/18. Working with teams weekly at check-ins.
Risk	Clinical Communication	Develop communication plan with clinical staff
Risk	Enterprise Communication	Develop communication plan with clinical

RAIDa Items
Risks
Issues
Decisions
Actions
0   5   10   15
○ Open ○ Closed

Data Center Build Out Metrics

Datacenter Build Out Burn Up
○ Completes Velocity ○ Theoretical Velocity ○ Planned Velocity

Datacenter Build Out Packages

On-Track	Equipment Package	Status	Planned Complete Date
○	Century Link SPW - TUK circuit	In Process	11/30/18
○	(1) Pure Storage FlashArray //X70	In Process	12/10/18
○	NetApp Filer - Quincy	Planning	12/18/18
○	11 UCS blades	Ready for Ins	12/20/18
○	F5 Loadbalancer - Quincy	Planning	12/22/18
○	Tenable Security Center	Backlog	12/29/18
○	(3) Isilon X410 / (3) NL410 nodes -	Backlog	12/30/18
○	(3) Isilon X410 / (3) NL410 nodes -	Backlog	12/30/18

Datacenter Build Out
62%
38%
○ Packages To Install ○ Packages Completed

Build Packages Progress By Steps
Backlog Planning Ready for Install In Process Complete

Application and Service Move Metrics

Application and Service Moves Burn Down
○ Completed Velocity ○ Theoretical Velocity ○ Planned Velocity

Applications and Services To Move

On-Track	Application	Status	Prod Move
○	3M ChartFactLocator Odessa Brown	In Process	12/25/18
○	Active Directory	In Process	12/31/18
○	StealthAudit	Planning	01/15/19
○	3M CGS - Core Grouping Software	Backlog	02/20/19
○	3M CRS - Coding & Reimbursement Systems	Backlog	03/07/19
○	Abacus	Backlog	04/01/19
○	Accellion Secure File Transfer	Backlog	04/12/19

Application and Service Moves
70%
30%
○ Items to Move ○ Moves Complete

Applications and Service Moves by Stages
Backlog Planning In Process Migrated Done

Budget Metrics

Budget v. Actual
$4,000
$3,000
$2,000
$1,000
$0
Yr 1 Q1 Yr 1 Q2 Yr 1 Q3 Yr 1 Q4 Yr 2 Q1 Yr 2 Q2 Yr 2 Q3 Yr 2 Q4
○ Budget ○ Actual

Total Variance
5%

Program Feedback

Program Feedback Received	Follow up info	Submitter Name First	Submitter Name Last	Created
I love my Ducks!	Me Too!	John	Franks	12/20/18 6:52 PM

Role of the Project Leader

The role of the project leader (PL) is anything but traditional in the ROPE framework. While many of the standard PM skills are required, the framework uses the multiplying force of coaching to allow analysts to manage much of the individual move tasks and activities. In fact, rather than the term PM we often refer to project leaders as coaches. In order to provide coaching, the PMs must be comfortable with the ROPE framework and the tasks in the move trains' workflow.

First and foremost, to off-load some of the traditional project management work from the PMs, the workstream manager owns reporting responsibilities and maintains project office artifacts. The tower leads work with the PMs as a team to establish mitigation for risk items identified by PMs as well as communicate status to senior leadership. The program manager owns the budget with input from the PMs.

With much of the traditional work lifted from the shoulders of the PMs, they are free to integrate into the application moves and guide them through the process. This includes:

- Provide training on the ROPE framework to teams of analysts and engineers.
- Provide communications and updates to their move teams.
- Work with analysts to ensure build sheet information is complete and accurate. Work with tower leads to incorporate individual build sheet information into the build sheet master. Work with analysts to resolve data anomalies.
- Work with analysts and engineers to develop a comprehensive cut sheet for each application migration.
- Provide back up for analysts at daily huddles.
- Maintain weekly check-ins with analyst teams to proactively remove obstacles, clear up confusions, manage staffing priorities and maintain focus on the migration effort.
- Work with analysts and engineers to maintain progress against the cut sheet.
- Remove and/or escalate roadblocks facing teams working through their cut sheet.
- Ensure adherence to move train processes, coaching team members (using job aids) on how to complete tasks or engage other teams.
- Perform go/no go reviews and ensure preparedness for move event.
- Run move event and gain sign off.

Typically, each PM works with a group of analysts under a logical grouping. This grouping is usually aligned to the analysts reporting structure. By aligning PMs to a group of analysts for the duration of their moves, the PM can establish a strong working relationship with these analysts and carry lessons learned across the teams.

Important skills for the coaching role are to know the move options available, understand how those options translate into tasks across the team, and possess strong facilitation skills in order to guide teams through the process.

Check-ins

Check-ins are weekly meetings that allow the PMs and analysts to catch up on project activities. It is recommended that these check-ins be incorporated into existing meetings with the team of analysts that are held by their supervisor or manager. By using a portion of an existing team meeting the following benefits are seen:

- Fewer meetings for analysts who have day to day customer responsibilities.
- Supervisor / manager gains insight about the datacenter move project from their staff.
- PMs gain firsthand understanding of analysts' responsibilities, conflicts and customer concerns outside the datacenter migration project.
- Builds a stronger sense of team between analysts and PM.

Most organizations have created teams of analysts that center around application or customer functionality. The project should utilize these organizational team lines to assign PMs and take advantage of existing team and relationship structures.

The check-ins should be a two-way conversation. PMs can provide information to the analysts about overall activities within the datacenter migration project, upcoming moves and lessons learned from other moves outside this team. It is also an opportunity for analysts to bring up questions and concerns that may need to be addressed at a larger scope than their individual moves.

The main goal of check-ins is to maintain an ongoing open dialog and build team work between analysts and PM. It cannot be over stated that these dialogs should be conducted live (preferably in person) rather than through email. If teams are geographically dispersed, it is recommended that initially the PM travel in order to establish a working relationship before settling into a remote based style using WebEx or Skype For Business to participate in discussions.

While we generally speak of applications and analysts, you can substitute service and engineers. Additionally, the PM focused on the engineering side of the project brings changes, improvements and lessons learned from the infrastructure teams to the analyst teams through their PMs.

Daily huddle

When an application analyst enters the daily huddles, the PM working with that analyst acts as a backup if the analyst is unable to attend a meeting. For this to be effective, the PM must remain current on the progress, issues, concerns and roadblocks of each application in their team's portfolio.

Since the PM is working actively with the analysts through the sprints, they will help guide analysts on which items should be brought to the daily huddle for resolution assistance and what other resources are available to assist.

A PM will be working with several analysts who are in various stages of sprint and attending the daily huddle. The PM needs to be intimate with all application move activities working through the sprint process for any of the analysts on the teams they are supporting.

Move Event

The move event is where the rubber meets the road and all the work in planning and pre-move pays off. The move events are a structured event and run in a very "NASA launch" manner to ensure the move tasks in the cut sheet are executed according plan.

During the move event the PM shifts hats and plays the role of "move master". The move master controls task execution and communication among the team during the move event in order to maintain measured progress and ensure success.

Because move events are occurring continually the micro move framework provides structure and guidance for these events.

At a high-level, the move event is a managed conference call / WebEx/ Skype for Business where all individuals involved in the event come together to execute their tasks. The move event also includes supporting engineers who may be required to assist if issues are encountered. While each move event may have some unique tasks, the flow and execution are repeatable across all move events.

Activities that build success

From start to finish, the framework builds to the move event for an application. It is important for the PM to participate in a coaching role with analysts along the way. This coaching role includes:

- Reviewing the build sheet information gather by analysts.
- Facilitating the development of cut sheets by analysts and engineers.
- Reviewing progress and participating in cut sheet task reviews.
- Lead the walk through of move event steps for go/no go readiness.

By actively participating and partnering with the analyst as a coach, the PM will become extremely familiar with the application move steps and be prepared to lead the application move event.

Build the cut sheet

Purpose: sets expectations, builds confidence, establishes confidence and removes barriers.

- Coach analysts
  - How to build a plan
  - Explain the cut sheet template
  - Communicate with participants
  - Review and refine drafts
  - Catch missing tasks
  - Check-off done tasks

- Explain the formal review process
  - Final review, not build the plan
  - Prep for formal review with all stakeholders involved

The analysts and engineers know and understand what to do in preparation and during the move. They may not appreciate how to lay out the tasks in a way that organizes the work together with the tasks of others. This is where the coaching skills of the PM come into play.

The framework does not ask for a Gantt or WBS for each application move. Instead using Smartsheet, the PM helps the analysts and engineers develop a simple check list of tasks to complete. These check list items are captured in the cut sheet which contains a task, who is going to complete the task and when it is due.

Starting with the cut sheet template the PM helps the analyst initially fill out the check list with items they know need to occur for their application. This may include getting a new license key for their application or bringing in the vendor to perform pre-move and move event tasks or work with specific users to build test files. The template will have common tasks such as communication, submitting change tickets and depending on the type of move, common infrastructure steps.

Once the initial draft cut sheet has been completed, the PM will work with the analyst to conduct a session with engineers, vendors and testers to walk through the draft and modify the cut sheet taking the draft version to a state where task owners agreed on their task details. The PMs will work with the analyst who should schedule weekly check-ins with the team members on the cut sheet to review progress and ensure completeness of the tasks.

In a best-case scenario, the draft version of the cut sheet is ready prior to sprint planning and finalized within the next few days.

Although the cut sheet is considered final, the team needs to understand that tasks may change over the next few weeks as lessons learned are collected from moving the lower environments or new information is uncovered.

PM's are encouraged to review the active application cut sheets daily and follow up with analysts suggesting any actions required to maintain velocity and ensure everyone is ready for the move event.

By staying involved in the details, without doing the work, a single PM can manage a portfolio of multiple applications in progress at any one time.

During the finalization of the cut sheet with the team, it is a good practice for the PM to review the move event process steps in order to set expectations. Also setting a date for the go/no go review is important to establish a sense of urgency as well as frame up the timeline for which all pre-move tasks need to be completed.

Above all, as a coach the PM needs to instill ownership of the move within the application analyst and supporting engineers.

Formal Go/No Go Cut Sheet Review

Formal cut sheet review

Purpose: *sets the tone for the move, gains buy-in and reassures business owner*

- Establish the flow
  - Explain the review process
  - Put focus on incomplete pre-tasks
  - Review move startup process and etiquette
  - Walk through technical cut over steps
  - Walk through testing steps
  - Walk through post steps
  - Walk through rollback
- Go / No Go
  - Steps all documented and ordered
  - Responsibilities assigned and accepted
  - Agreement the move can process on target

The formal review is one of the last and most important tasks prior to the move event. The formal review has several intents including:

- Validate pre-move steps have been completed. Any pre-move tasks that have not been completed should be discussed as to the reason for their incompleteness and commitment that they will be completed or note them if they are no longer required.

- Gain buy-in from everyone involved that they agree the task list for the move event is complete, ordered correctly and if executed according to the cut sheet, will produce successful results. Everyone who has a task (analysts, engineers, testers, DBAs, …) need be in the review to give a "go". Any "no go" should be discussed and every effort given to doing what it takes to achieve a go. For example: QA may say no go because the baseline testing was not completed. However, the tester has committed to having the baseline testing completed and documented by the end of the day. At the opening of the move event a final go/no go will be taken to ensure all issues and concerns have been resolved from the final review.
- For extremely complex or critical applications, the customers (business owner) should be invited to ensure they are comfortable with the move event of their applications. For less critical applications the business owner may give their proxy to the application analyst.

The review is a dress rehearsal, and as such the move master (the PM) conducts the review announcing each step and asking for confirmation of correctness. Everything about the review is to draw out any last-minute concerns, build confidence and set expectations.

Move Event

Move event
Purpose: *orderly move of an application following the cut sheet's technical, testing and steps*

- **Establish the flow**
  - Explain the move protocol
  - Verify completeness of all pre-tasks
  - Roll call, including NOC.
  - Use NOC to reach out if needed
  - Start on time but not before
- **Migration**
  - Walk through technical and testing steps
  - Follow protocol
  - Maintain control – know when to shut it down
- **Go / No Go**
  - Agreement the move is complete

The move event protocol is the result of numerous refinements over the years and has proved successful across all industries. Since there are several resources on the call, some for the first time, it is important to review protocol at the start of the move event call. The protocol has the following components:

- Move master is in charge and controls conversations and actions. Everyone should be on mute while not talking.
- There should be a second PM as a backup for the move master. The backup should listen for concerns and provide information to the move master as needed. The backup PM should use an IM session to communicate with the move master in order to relate concerns and information. The backup PM may temporarily take on the move master role if the move master needs a break. The move master will take back control upon their return to the call. There is one person in charge of the call and that is the move master.
- Call for the move event opens 15 minutes prior to the start of the move event. Everyone with tasks for the move must dial into the call.
- The cut sheet for the move is displayed for everyone to see and follow along.
- Ten minutes prior to the move event a rollcall is conducted with each person responding "go" or "no go". If a resource is not on the call for rollcall, have them paged out. If a non-critical resource does not respond to the page their "go" is assumed. A non-critical resource might be a supervisor who felt they needed to be invited. Testers are expected to be on the call at the start. If they fail to show within 30 minutes of paging their tests are assumed successful and their go accepted.
- For each task the move master will call out the name of the person and ask them to execute their step, reading the step. The individual needs to respond (confirm) so the move master knows they heard them. And the move master confirms their acknowledgement. When the task is complete the person responsible will call out the task is complete, and the move master will confirm receipt of the completed task and check the task as complete in the cut sheet. The move master will proceed to the next task. This back and forth is essential to ensure everyone on the call is aware of progress and avoid issues when folks are talking on mute thinking the move master heard them.
- If a task requires a significant amount of time to complete, the move master should ask for an update every 5 – 10 minutes to keep the group informed.
- When the move master reaches the testing tasks, the QA representative should assume command, allowing testers to begin, guide the activities between testers and collect sign off. When testing is complete the QA representative provides the collective go for all testers.
- If an issue is detected during testing, the move master notes it in the issue log and assigns it to an individual to work. Critical issues must be resolved before the move event is complete and may initiate a rollback if it cannot be resolved. Minor issues such as printers needing to be

restarted may be completed the following day and the move considered successful.

- When engineers and analysts are working through an issue, allow them to openly discuss the issue on the call. The move master should avoid giving too much direction to the technical staff but know when to rein it back in if they appear to be going down a rabbit hole. If the technical staff is stuck, ask open ended questions to stimulate their thinking about why the application may have this issue.

- Rollback decision is made by the move master. It is his or her responsibility to collect information from the various stakeholders, weighting them appropriately, to make the call. During any time spent trying to resolve issues, the move master should poll stakeholders to understand the criticality of the issue, gauge impact to users and gain consensus to keep going wherever possible.

- After the application is moved and tested, a final go/no go is held to ensure everyone agrees the application move is complete. Review any post-move tasks that are required and end the call.

- At the end of the call, the application move is considered complete and support responsibility is rolled over to operations.

The slide below summarizes the important points we've discussed concerning the move event protocol. This slide is often displayed at the opening of the move event call and used to walk everyone through the protocol before going into rollcall.

Guidelines of move call protocol

These guidelines help set the tone of the call allowing you to smoothly progress through the cut over event. The guide represent lessons learned from hundreds of moves for numerous clients.

Mute Your Phone

There are a lot of folks on the call please mute your phone. Don't forget to unmute when its your turn to speak.

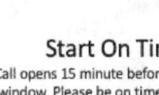

Start On Time

Call opens 15 minute before the change window. Please be on time for role call and last minute review.

Silence is not golden

On long tasks take a check point every 15 minutes to make sure it's still on track. Just a quick check on progress.

I Got This

Call confirmation for task start & end. Request a response for each handoff. Let everyone know who's got this.

30 Minute Rule

No show = positive agreement. Lots of people are involved in a cut over event. Waiting costs time and money.

NOC Is Our Friend

Your eyes and ears into everything going on across the enterprise. The NOC will call out to others as needed.

Team Effort

Everyone starts and ends the cut over event call together. No man left behind... or leaves early.

There Is Only One

I'm your move master I will be directing your call this evening. One leader, move master is it on the call.

The critical move step

Purpose: everyone comes together to move the application and test

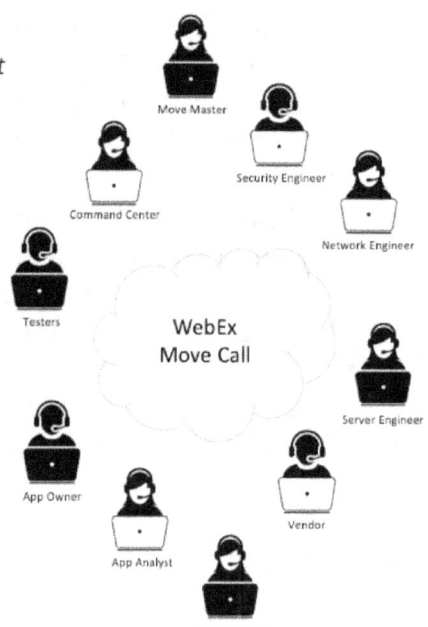

- Everyone dials into the move call
- Move master orchestrates the call tasks
- Cut sheet steps executed as reviewed
- Testers validate the app after move
- Issues tracked and resolved on the call
- Everyone agrees on move success
- Handoff to ongoing operations
- Call ends on schedule

Move events bring together a large amount of resources to ensure a successful outcome. For example: an analyst requested firewall rule changes to be ready prior to the move event. Although the security engineer should not be required to perform work during the move event, they are on the call in case there is trouble with the rule. The same holds true for networking engineers who may have built VIPs or configured port settings.

Anyone who may be needed on the call to resolve an issue or possible issue, is on the call from the start. The idea is that every effort be made to fall forward rather than rollback. Having engineers on the call who can help isolate and resolve the issue saves significant time spent paging on-call engineers who are not familiar with the application and move.

The move master may need to have an engineer paged out and should utilize the NOC / Service Desk to page or call the required resource.

One question that often occurs in the middle of calls is: "Hey I'm done, can I leave now". We prefer to keep people on the call. If rollback is required, they will undo what they just did. If testers don't want to watch engineers move the app, remind them that engineers must watch them test the app. It can be difficult, but the preference is for everyone to join the call from the start and leave at the finish. This is a team effort.

The project leader plays several key roles in ROPE framework. As the analysts and engineers go through the process several times, they will find their groove and the pace of application moves will pick up.

There are times when multiple application moves will be scheduled at the same time or closely overlapping times. We have found that a single call bridge call (Skype for Business or WebEx) can support up to five individual moves occurring at the same time. The key to successfully managing multiple application move events at the same time, on the same bridge is for the move master to have reviewed all the application cut sheets prior to the move and maintain clear communications on the call as to who is performing which task for which application move.

If a difficult issue arises for one of the applications on a multi-application move call, a second bridge call may be opened. The team designated to work on the issue should move to the new bridge call. The backup PM should move to the new bridge call with the engineers and provide move master support on the call until the issue is resolved and everyone rejoins the original move call. The two move masters should instant message or text status back and forth so teams on both calls remain updated.

Databases

Databases are a bit unique and can cause confusion when it comes to moving. We have found that typical organizations have a variety of database management systems (DBMS) including: MS SQL, MySQL, Oracle, Cassandra and others. These different DBMS are typically on a mix of infrastructure with their own strengths and constraints. Inevitably some databases will be physical while others are on virtual servers. Some are clustered, others are on stand-alone servers.

At the database level, most of the complexity is the result of shared databases. While applications can move independent of their database, when shared databases are moved, all applications with a database on that shared database system are affected. The coordination and communication required to move a shared database can be daunting.

There are a couple of points to consider when moving databases:

- If a database is on a physical server, virtualizing it can significantly reduce the downtime impact. Many physical databases can be easily virtualized provided the virtual resources are available.
- Oracle licenses its DBMS based on CPU/Proc counts. It views the entire virtual environment when counting CPU/Procs, not simply the virtual server that the Oracle database will run on. Setting up a separate virtual environment with limited resources may be required to fulfill licensing agreements in order to virtualize.
- Clustered nodes can be paused and moved one at a time. It is important that all devices in the cluster be on the same OS and patch release in order to prevent unknown behaviors as you bring resources in and out of the cluster.
- In cases where clusters have been collapsed to a single node it is important to recognize there is still a quorum drive. When the node is moved the DBMS will want to fail over and in a single node case may cause the quorum drive to be locked out preventing the DBMS from coming back up.
- Rollback can be complex for shared databases when all applications initially test out fine. Occasionally, post-move usage of the applications will find an application is working, but in a degraded state. Plan for falling forward by identifying and resolving the source of the degradation or failing back a single database rather than the entire shared DBMS if possible.
- While clustering for MS SQL is not new, pre-2012 MS SQL version tends to cause more issues with cluster moves than 2012 and above versions.
- Access DB is usually not supported by IT/IS and most likely is frowned upon because of security concerns. Nevertheless, many users will have Access databases tucked away on files shares and they consider them

essential to the business workflow. In the case of unsupported databases, it is important to communicate out to the owners what will change (move their file share causing a name change in their connector), when it is changing, what may break and any resources available to assist. Don't take ownership of unsupported DBMS, instead provide as much communication and notices as possible so that the owners can mitigate any issues.

Databases require trained resources to ensure data integrity during a move. While DBAs may not have moved datacenters before, they have likely moved their databases from server to server many times. Rely on their expertise to develop a solid cut sheet plan on how to move the databases they are responsible for. Databases should be treated like an application. They can move independent of the application(s) that connect to them. It will be up to the DBA and the application analyst to determine the most effective time(s) to move the database.

Build Sheets

The idea of a build sheet developed from a need to bridge communications across analysts, server engineers, network engineers, DBAs, business users, security engineers and others. The build sheet needs to communicate the current As-Is state of the application to everyone.

A problem we found is that each group views the datacenter move, or any complex technology project for that matter, from their domain's perspective. Business users and analysts think in terms of the application name. DBAs know the name of their database. Server engineers think in terms of host names while the network team focuses on IP addresses with security wanting to drill down to port and protocol. The build sheet was designed to bring these core elements into one location in order to facilitate a communication about an application across all groups.

Before going further and discussing the elements of the build sheet, it is important to understand what the build sheet is not. The build sheet is not the all-encompassing data repository for every aspect of the application and its supporting infrastructure. We have witnessed organizations which spent months, even years collecting and recording data about applications and servers in order to figure out how to group applications and satisfy every groups' desire to have their information maintained. The difficulties with an all-encompassing data repository for everything application, server and network are:

- A small army is required to maintain integrity of a large data repository.
- The move project is not the best source of record for most data.
- The mass of data becomes a source of contention rather than a useful tool.
- An enterprise CMDB (configuration management database) is a better source repository for all things CI (configuration item).

If your organization has a complete and accurate CMDB, the work for creating build sheets can be as simple as generating some reports. If not, investigation by the application analysts is required to document the required information. The build sheet is one of the most important tools to get correct for a successful application move and there are no real short cuts to the effort involved in identifying the servers and their interfaces.

Each build sheet is a Smartsheet focused on one application. Since the build sheet is in a spreadsheet format rather than a relational database, some data will be repeated on multiple rows in order to facilitate filtering and allow all build sheets to be rolled up into a build sheet master (a searchable, master set of all build sheet information collated together). Items in the build sheet break down into two categories: core application and application interfaces.

Core application information:

The core application information is usually easy for the application analyst to assemble. This information is common and can be easily recorded by anyone familiar with the technical support details of the application.

The table below describes the core information portion of the build sheet and describes the data to collect.

Column header	Description
ID	The ID associated with the application. Typically, this comes from the CMDB or other authoritative list of applications. The ID is used to tie the build sheet back to the authoritative list and provide clarity when an application is known by more than one name.
Environment	Drop down list: • Production • Dev • Test • QA • HA • Other (describe) All the environments for a single application should be represented in a single build sheet.
Cut Sheet Owner	Enter the name of the person (application analyst) who supports the application or database. This is the person responsible for technical implementation as well as care and feeding of the application on a day to day basis.
Application Name	Name of the application or database. This should match up to the CMDB or other authoritative list of applications.
Host name Internal	A-name of the server associated with the application or database. You can use the DNS Record to get the A-record and IP address. "nslookup -type=A <<server name>>" replace <<server name>> with host name you are looking up.

Column header	Description
Server IP Address	IP address associated with the application or database servers. You can use the DNS Record to get the A-record and IP address.

"nslookup -type=A <<server name>>" replace <<server name>> with host name you are looking up. |
| Server Type | Drop drown list:

- Virtual
- Physical
- Appliance |
| Server Category | Identify if it is a:

- Web server
- Database server
- Terminal Server
- App Server

Put in as many as apply when services are combined on the same server. |
| Load Balancer or Master IP for Failover - VIP | Load Balancer or Master IP for Failover – VIP. Allows infrastructure engineers to know the service that needs to move (or built new) for the application. |
| VLAN | VLAN where server resides. This is required if you are stretching layer 2 between datacenters in order to know what will be affected when VLAN gateways are migrated. |

Application Interface information

As mentioned earlier, interface information is one of the most important items to understand about an application. It is also the one area that most organizations know the least about. The movement of an application impacts applications and services interfacing with the application. Knowing those impacts is what allows everyone to plan for, accurately communicate impacts and test appropriately when an application moves.

As analysts begin to fill in their build sheets, they need to pay attention to the interfaces. More post-move issues are the result of missed interface connections than anything else. It is particularly important to identify connections that external clients may have through VPN, jump boxes or other devices where firewall rules must be considered and setup prior to the move. When identifying server to server connections, analysts only need to go to the next hop. They do not need to document the full path of communication for their entire workflow. For example:

  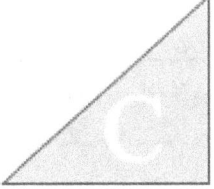

When following a "Like for Like" move principle, if application "A" connects to interface engine "B" in order to talk with database "C":

- Analyst for application "A" will document "B" as its interface.
- Analyst for interface engine "B" will document "A" and "C" as its interfaces.
- Analyst for database "C" will document "B" as its interface.

The reason for settling on this level of interface documentation is that when "A" moves, "C" should not require changes or testing. Both "A" and "C" are affected when "B" changes and only "B" will need to be tested as "C" moves.

In the build sheet analysts need to replicate rows of core application information to account for each of the interfaces that one server may have.

Column Header	Description
Server to Server Interface Name	Enter the name of the interface. Interfaces will often have standard naming conventions that describe the origin and destination for the information. Repeat this information for all lines associated with the interface. FTP servers for example.
Interface hostname	A-name of the server associated with the interface application or database. You can use the DNS Record to get the A-record and IP address. "nslookup -type=A <<server name>>" replace <<server name>> with host name you are looking up.

Column Header	Description
Interface IP/Host ID	IP address associated with the interface application or database servers or servers. You can use the DNS Record to get the A-record and IP address. "nslookup -type=A <<server name>>" replace <<server name>> with host name you are looking up.
Interface Type	Enter the type (direction) of interface (drop down): • Input • Output • Bidirectional
Interface Port	Identify the port used by the interface to communicate. For example, typically: • HTTP traffic uses port 80. • HTTPS traffic uses port 443. • FTP traffic uses port 21. • SFT traffic uses port 22. • SSH traffic uses port 22. • MS SQL traffic uses port 1433.
Data Protocol	Identify the protocol used to communicate over the interface. For example: • HTTP • HTTPS • FTP • SFTP • SQL • Vendor proprietary
VLAN Where Interface Resides	VLAN where interface server exits. Important in determining outages when stretch layer 2 is in place and VLAN gateway swings occur.
Notes	Use for any notes you would like to capture information about the application or its move.

Some individuals who review the build sheet may believe additional columns are required to retain pertinent information about the application, server or environment. This may be true, however, before adding a column ask the following questions.

- Who is the information for?
- Who can provide the information?
- Is the information easily available and can it be found by using the information already in the build sheet?
- What value does the information communicate to other teams?

For example:

"We need to record OS patch level, so the server engineer knows which script to set up for the move."

In this case the information is for the server engineer who is the only one needing it. The server engineer is also the person to provide the information. Additionally, the information may change month to month.

Rather than gather the information and record it in the build sheet, a better solution is to have the server engineer, who will use the host name / IP to cue up the servers for the move, check the OS patch level at that time and set up the move using the appropriate script.

While this is a simple example it is more often the case that using the IP / host name, engineers, DBAs and analysts can go directly to the servers, applications, or databases in question and find the information needed at the time it is needed. The interface information directs them to the servers that will be affected so they can validate information on them as well when it is time to prepare for the move.

The build sheet should contain the least amount of information needed to convey the current As-Is state. The goal is for all staff members to gather any additional relevant information they may need for themselves based on the shared information in the build sheet. The idea of "less is more" cannot be over stated here. Don't turn your datacenter migration into a massive data gathering project.

Build sheet master

The power of the build sheet is in its simplicity. The build sheet master takes that simplicity and multiplies its value. Once all the build sheets are complete, the build sheet master is assembled from all the individual sheets becoming an accumulation of all rows across all sheets. With all the rows of servers and interfaces in one place, you can now cross reference information across all applications, databases, servers and interfaces. Once set up, the Smartsheet version of the build sheet master can automatically pull in build sheet records and updates into the build sheet master in real-time.

As you recall in the build sheet, analysts documented their immediate interface. The build sheet master can now show the complete communication path for the entire work flow.

For example:

  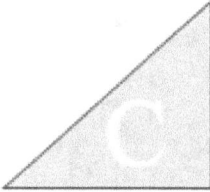

If application "A" connects to application "B" which talks with shared database "C":

- Application "A" build sheet will document "B" as its interface.
- Application "B" build sheet will document "A" and "C" as its interfaces.
- Database "C" build sheet will document "B" as its interface.

The build sheet master can be filtered or pivoted to show applications "A", "B" and "C" are communicating in a work flow. The build sheet master lets you validate impacts across applications and answer many of the questions customers have when planning down times. These questions include:

- What is affected when we move the gateway for VLAN "XYZ"? Apps and databases that are in VLAN "XYZ" as well as any that communicate with them.
- What is affected when we move shared database "C"? Apps that interface directly with database "C" and apps that interfaces to those apps.

The build sheet master is typically owned by the application tower lead who will regularly use it to validate with PMs and analysts that all components for the cut sheet have been covered as well as help PMs and analyst determine communication requirements for all impacted customers. The build sheet master will also assist QA in identifying testing requirements.

Cut Sheets

With most large organizations, the application and service move count will run 500 plus. If you are not a project manager, you probably don't enjoy building schedules in MS Project or analyzing Gantt charts for critical path. The question becomes how do you schedule and maintain 500 plus moves without an army of project managers? The answer is check lists.

Everyone understands a check list. Walk down the aisles of any IT team and you will most likely find white boards with a list of items technical staff are working on. These tasks or check lists are how most technical staff manage their assigned non-project work. The cut sheet takes advantage of the technical staff's existing use of check lists to self-manage their work.

The cut sheet is a schedule, disguised as a checklist. The advantage of the cut sheet over everyone's individual white board is that it has everyone's tasks on it for the pre-move, move and Post-move activities. The information for tasks on the cut sheet is purposely kept simple:

Column name	Description
Done	A check box indicating the task is complete. A format rule should be set to cross out the task when the check box is checked to visually indicate the line item is complete and reinforce the team's momentum.
Task Name	A short description of the task such as "arrange for vendor participation" or "submit change control" or "create VIP". "The Checklist Manifesto" by Atul Gawande is a good resource to assist in achieving the appropriate level of detail.
Comments	Free form additional information that may be important to the task owner. For example: "old VIP at 10.10.100.231 on NetScaler, new VIP to be created on F5 in DMZ" or "John Smith is vendor account manager, Sandy Jones is engineer supporting the account. New SOW required". These notes can be as detailed as needed or left blank if the task is fully understood by the person responsible for the task.
Assigned To	The person responsible for completing the task. This can be a bit controversial in the case when

	several people will be involved in completing a task. The Assigned To individual needs to be the primary person who becomes responsible for following up with all others to get the entire task completed.
	By assigning the task to one person you cut down the number of tasks where each person does a small piece and force one person to own responsibility to the entire deliverable. Be clear with the Assigned To individual that they own driving the task to completion through others if this is the case and not simply reporting that another person is delaying the task completion.
Duration	This column is used for move event tasks to assist with timing. Generally, this will be in minutes. By summing up the task durations in the move event section, the team can determine the length of outage required and create a change control to cover the appropriate timing.
	Duration can be used for any task in the cut sheet, however, you should be driving to dates and placing responsibility on the task owner to start early enough to complete on time.
Due Date	Date the task needs to be complete.

Done Color code	Task Name Mile Stone	Comments Migration Event Start / End	Due Date Not Required	start time Fall Back Tasks	Assigned To (responsib Contacts emergency phone #	Inform on completion	Accountable manager
Instruc-tions	Move Diagram is attached on column 1 This template provides an outline for building a Cut Sheet to migrate a specific application. Entries have been placed in the template to remind creators of key tasks that should be included on all Cut Sheets. Begin by entering your migration event Start Date in row 5 below. This will populate other dates to help schedule your application move sprint.	File Name - Save the Cut Sheet using the following name: "Cut Sheet - <application name><D/Q/P> <##>" Where D = dev system, Q = QA/testing system, P = production system. Replace ## with a unique two digit number Use "Discussions" rather than email where possible. Attach files to specific rows as needed to support tasks	When must this task be completed in order to move the application on the migration event date?	Use a 24 hour clock. Only required for the migration event. Used to verify the change window and provide fall back check points.	Individual responsible for completing this tasks	Who do you need to inform so that they can begin their work?	Which manager is accountable if the task is not complete. This is an escalation path if needed.
	CHER		08/12/15		Kent T	Jean Stanton	Susan Moore
	Build Sheet review and tweaks	Review build sheet with infrastructure team. Make any modifications necessary	06/15/15		Kent Right		Susan Moore
	Pre-Migration tasks	all tasks that need to be completed leading up to the application migration event					
	New Virtual Server Build initiated at DCA for application	objcyc02 (with CName objcyc)	07/15/15		IT - MSS Distro List		
	Kick Off	Quick meeting (lync call) with all involved to start the sprint. Re-validate Migration Date.	07/15/15		Kent Right		Susan Moore
	2 week prior communication	Follow communication plan notifying business, vendors, teams of migration.	07/22/15		Kent Right		Susan Moore
	Review Cutsheet with Infrastructure, customer, business	Make sure everyone still agrees on cut sheet plan and nothing has changed.	07/25/15		Kent Right		Susan Moore
	Submit Change Control	Follow GH Change control process use the DCAM template	07/27/15		Kent Right		Susan Moore
	<Create server infrastructure service tickets>	Request for server, objcyc02	07/29/15 07/29/15		Kent Right		Bob Johnson
	2 week prior communication	Follow communication plan notifying business, vendors, teams of migration.	07/31/15		Kent Right		Susan Moore
	New IP Address assigned to Server	10.2.22.21	07/31/15		IT - MSS Distro List		
	Execute CHER Validation Plan against baseline in Tukwila.		07/31/15		Kent Right		Susan Moore
	Create Ticket to backup server	objCyc02 Ticket REQ0043444	08/01/15		Kent Right		Susan Moore
	Folders created on server		08/02/15		Kent Right		Susan Moore
	Permissions assigned to folders on server		08/02/15		Kent Right		Susan Moore
	Validate Environment Set up		08/05/18		Kent Right		Susan Moore
	1 week prior communication	Follow communication plan notifying business, vendors, teams of migration.	08/07/15		Kent Right		Susan Moore
	Pre-Migration Go/No Go decision		08/09/15		Kent Right		Susan Moore
	CHER Application Migration	Prod System	08/12/15 12:00PM Noon				
	Open conference call - join conference call bridge 15 minutes prior to roll call	<con call info goes here>		11:45PM	Move Master		
	Take final Go/No Go role call	Jill - go, Jean - go, Kent go, Purnima - go, Roger - go		12:55PM	Move Master		
	Send out start Communication	Start Application Migration		12:00	Kent Right		
	Migration steps			12:00			
	Stop CHER interfaces and have message queue up on message broker. Wait for notification that cname objcyc is pointing to new address			12:00	Roger Lester	LIS_Team@abc.com	
	Change folder location of HL7 message within the Maintenance Tool.			12:05	Kent Right		Susan Moore
	Final replication of D: drive files to new server			12:15PM	Jill Lincon		
	Change DNS to point CNAME 'objcyc' to new server 'objcyc02' in DCA			12:20PM	Jill Lincon	Kent Right	IT - MSS Distro List
	Inform team that CName has shifted.			12:30PM	Jill Lincon	LIS_Team@abc.com	IT - Interface Engine
	Inform Interface Engine Team that CNAME 'objcyc' has shifted to Quincy and that objcyc is ready to receive HL7 messages. CHER execution group may now be 'bounced'.			12:40PM	Kent Right	IT_Interface@abc.com	Susan Moore
	Bounce CHER execution group to update cached cname info.			12:45PM	Roger Lester		
	Start CHER interfaces to resume CHER processing			12:50PM	Roger Lester	Kent Right	Susan Moore
	Testing Activities						
	Validate that HL7 messages are flowing and that the CHER tables are being updated.			1:00PM	Purnima Smith	IT - Interface Engine	Susan Moore
	Point CHER UI to new server location			1:05PM	Kent Right		
	Validate messages can be opened in CHER User Interface			1:15PM	Kent Right		Susan Moore
	Developer executes CHER Validation Plan	Attach test plan. adjust time required to complete testing.		1:20PM	Kent Right		
	Customer Testing	Attach User test plan. adjust time required to complete testing.		1:20PM	Jean Stanton	Kent Right	Jean Stanton
	Customer Approval to Go Live	<Link to issue list sheet> All blocking issues resolved. See issues list for any follow up items not stopping Go Live		2:00PM	Kent Right		Susan Moore
	Send Notification that all sites are up to application owners	<distribution list for email notification> <upload email to send out>		2:00PM	Kent Right		Susan Moore
	EQA Approval				Annie Pattel		
	Confirm end of conference call and hand off to support	Roger - go, Jill - go, cs, Kent - Go, Purnima - Go, Jean -go.	08/12/15 6:00PM				
	Post implementation Day 1 tasks	Task to complete following the migration go live.					
	Decommission objcyc (old) server	Kent to open ticket for MSS to decom.	09/12/15		Jill Lincon		
	Fall Back Plan	Notes about fallback. Call out if there is a point at which cannot fall back and must go forward.					
	Bring down Interface Engine				Roger Lester		
	Change DNS to point back at the AMB server; reverse CNAME change				Jill Lincon		
	Repoint UI to objcyc.				Kent Right		
	Bring original server back online, resume replication.				IT - MSS Distro List	Kent Right	
	Send Notification to users & project contacts that changes were backed out.	We are live on original server			Kent Right		Susan Moore

Contact List	Primary emergency phone #	Cell	Group/Role
Susan Moore	226-922-7922		Manager
Kent Right	622-5662 (226-922-5662)	362-932-6662	Analyst
Roger Lester (Interface Engine Team)	226-442-4969 (322-4969)/C 499-773-2793		Message Broker
Jean Stanton (Primary user - Transcription Services)	226-922-9973 (822-9973)		End User
Amy Johnson	226-326-4322		End User Tester
Purnima Smith	W: 226-442-2636/C 469-226-6255		EQA

As mentioned, the cut sheet has several sections, each with different purposes and expectations. The sections of a cut sheet are:

- Pre-move tasks
- Move event tasks

- Post-move tasks
- Fall back tasks
- Contact list

We have found a simple color code assists everyone in recognizing key items in the cut sheet. Milestone items are color coded orange. Milestones or important events include reviews, communications, CAB reviews or rows with key elements such as start testing.

The start and end of the move event are signified by a green row. Every task in between the two green rows must be completed to call the move complete.

The fall back plan is highlighted in light red. The contact list is highlighted in light blue. The highlighting allows individuals to quickly get to either of these two areas if needed.

Our template also includes items highlighted in light yellow indicating required fields as well as fields highlighted in grey indicating no data required. As the done box is checked, the text in the row turns light grey and struck through to indicate it is complete.

We also recommend the move master highlight any items they feel necessary during the final go/no go review. The highlights should be used alongside with the comments field to remind the move master of any special instructions or items that need to be called out or coordinated by them during the move event.

One caution on colors and highlighting. Too many highlighted rows distract from the importance of any highlighted row. Keep highlights and colors to a minimum.

Pre-move Tasks

Pre-move tasks are the tasks leading up to the move event that need to be completed before an application or service can successfully move to the new datacenter. These are generally kept to a high level, often including a couple of sub-tasks to complete. The tasks in the pre-move section should be deliverable oriented and are typically well understood by the task owner. For example: Create VIP - Network engineers know how to create a VIP and understand they will need the new server IP addresses from the server team as well as prepare for a DNS record change.

The goal for the pre-move section is not to create an exhaustive list of detailed tasks but rather to ensure all deliverables required are assembled and ready for the move event.

Several of the deliverables in the pre-move section should be common and included in the base template. Common tasks include:

- Present at sprint planning.
- Engage vendor.

- Create tickets for: VIP, firewall rules, VPN change, ...
- Submit and receive change control approval.
- Finalize cut sheet.
- Send out communication #1.
- Send out communication #2.
- Send out communication #3.
- Go/no go review.
- Set up move event call.
- Build/validate test plan.
- Run baseline test.

As many common tasks as possible should be added to the cut sheet template[7] at the appropriate level of detail required to ensure completeness. Task that are not required for a particular application or service move should be deleted by the analyst as they go through and tailor the cut sheet for their move.

Move Event Tasks

The tasks that occur during the move event are detailed. This section should be every step or hand off required to complete the move. The duration of these tasks is usually in minutes. The completeness of one task will usually govern the start of the next step. The detail level of the move events ensures no detail is forgotten or missed by the team performing the move. The detail also allows the change board or customer reviewing the details to be confident that the team has thought through all the tasks and hand offs required to execute a successful move of the application.

Example of tasks in the move event section include:

- Place server into maintenance mode in monitoring system.
- Stop application.
- Stop application database.
- Shut down server.
- Complete final copy of data.
- Perform application validation tests.
- ...

The team needs to walk through these steps a number of times to ensure a complete list of tasks has been documented, the order is correct, and the durations are reasonably accurate. If move event tasks have hard dependencies, they should be called out in the comments section. If multiple tasks can run in parallel, they should be identified in the comments section. The goal is to ensure everyone knows the flow of work that will occur and by

---

[7] See included cut sheet template example.

who during the move event. In general, this section is reviewed several times during the sprint check-ins to validate no tasks have been missed and cement the order of execution. The reviews should be performed as a group that includes everyone who has a task.

Generally engineering tasks will be common for all moves of the same type (V2V, P2V, ...) and can be templatized then pasted into individual cut sheets. This aids in building a complete set of move event tasks and can improve the cut sheets over time as tasks are adjusted from lessons learned or automation is applied to engineering tasks.

The final "go/no go review" of the cut sheet will gain everyone's agreement on the steps, order and timings. If done correctly this review is with the business owner or customer, and it is a simple review with no last-minute changes or additions.

Post-move tasks

Tasks that occur after the move event is declared successful fall into the post-move section of the cut sheet. These tasks are generally considered cleanup. Tasks that fall into this category include:

- Create decommission ticket to remove old server.
- Remove old server from monitoring.
- Update CMDB configuration items with new addresses.
- Validate backups ran successful.

These tasks are important and need to be completed but may occur over the next few days following a successful move and need not be part of the actual move event.

Fall Back tasks

While no one plans to fail it is important to consider how the application will fall back if the move event cannot be completed within the planned time or does not pass testing and cannot be fixed within the scheduled time frame.

In some cases, these tasks will be a simple reversal of the move steps. In other cases, completely different steps will need to be taken to account for changes in data that may have occurred in downstream applications. Regardless of how simple or complicated, the fall back plan should be as detailed as the steps in the actual move event.

The most difficult part of a move can be deciding if and when to execute the fall back. Time checks should be in the move event task list to validate the activity is running on time as well as any points that would significantly increase the difficulty of the rollback. At these junctures, a pause should be taken to ensure everyone is in agreement to continue forward.

During the move event it is important to have a customer representative who can make critical decisions. For example: A move maybe taking longer than expected and the team has reached the time to fail back. The move master should reach out to the customer representative in order for them to choose if it is possible to allow a longer downtime for the team to complete the move. Other times a small issue may not test correctly, such as one of three printers is not responding, and the customer representative can allow the application to remain in the new datacenter with follow up the next day.

The goal is to fail forward if possible.

Contact list

The contact list contains everyone who may be required for the move event. The list includes everyone expected to be on the conference bridge as well as those who may need to be called in for support if required. Unless the probability of needing a resource for support is considered extremely low, all resources should be attending the call.

The contact number should be a phone or cell phone that the person can be reached at off hours and not their desk phone.

In some organizations the NOC has an afterhours contact sheet for all technical resources and you can rely on the NOC to contact them if needed. In any case, you should be able to contact the following during any part of the move event:

- Application analysts.
- Technical resources and their backups.
- Testers.
- Vendors.
- Technology manufacturers' service desk.
- Customer / business decision maker.
- Project sponsor.
- NOC or operations center.

If individuals need to be contacted, ask the NOC/operations center, who should be on the move event call, to page/call out the individual and ask them to join the move event bridge line. Be sure the NOC has all the information needed for the person to join the bridge. If your organization does not have a NOC the backup PM should use the contact list to reach out to the required individual.

Base level infrastructure tasks

Each type of move has infrastructure tasks that are consistent. It is extremely helpful to have these tasks documented so that they can be copied and pasted into an application's cut sheet by the application analyst.

After the "Move Method Options" document is approved, the infrastructure tower lead works with the infrastructure leads from each domain to develop the repetitive tasks they need to complete for each move. An example of a virtual move using VEEAM where the IP address is changing might be:

- Server team
  - Pre-move
    - Assign new IP address(s)
    - Validate VM(s) readiness (patched, version)
    - Initial copy started
    - Initial copy complete and validated
    - Start server synch process
    - Validate health of synch process
    - Adjust frequency of synch process
  - Move
    - Remove server(s) from monitoring
    - Power off server(s)
    - Start final sync script
    - Update IP and host name
    - Reset MAC address
    - Power on servers
    - Validate NIC and check services
    - Adjust System time
    - Hand off server(s) to application team
  - Post-move
    - Place server(s) back into monitoring
    - Decommission old VM(s)

Depending on the level of automation, tools, and engineering experience the number of steps may change. The goal is to have a set of steps that are repetitive for each type of move so that they can be pasted into the cut sheet.

With the infrastructure steps known and pasted into the cut sheet, the analyst can then add other steps around these such as bring the application down, bring the database down, ...

For each type of move there are typically repeatable tasks required from all the infrastructure teams including, network, security, compute, storage, identity management, ...

You should view these steps under the lens of the 80/20 rule. Eighty percent of the time the steps will apply but the infrastructure teams must participate in walks of the cut sheet to identify unique situations and steps that comprise the illusive twenty percent.

The following represents a list of common infrastructure tasks associated with application moves that should have standardized steps:

- Network
  - Load Balancer (VIP)
  - VPN connections
- Security
  - Firewall rules
  - Security zones
- Compute
  - Server moves virtual
  - Sever moves physical
- Storage
  - Data copy
  - SAN connectivity
  - NAS connections
  - Backups

Tech Info Sheet

The tech info sheet contains the To-Be that is a reference to participating engineers and analysts during the move event. The tech info sheet should contain columns of To-Be information that participants may need to reference or pass between each other as they work through the pre-move, move and Post-move tasks.

There is one row for each server to be moved. The following table represents common tech sheet rows but may be augmented with additional columns for any items that are required to change. The information in the tech info sheet should be added during the pre-move tasks as items are assigned. It should be complete prior to the move go/no go review and quickly scanned during the review to validate readiness

Column name	Description
Old Host Name	Anchors the row back to original server name from the build sheet
Old IP Address	Anchors the row back to the original server address from the build sheet
New Host Name	If the host names are changing the new name of the server should be present. This information may be used by networking to create a DNS alias or new FQN entry if required. This information should be made available as soon as possible.
New IP Address	If the IP addresses are changing the new address of the server should be present. This information will be required by several participants and should be made available as soon as possible.
New Load Balancer (VIP) IP address and name	Allows analysts to test VIPs using IP address and host files prior to the move event.
New DNS entries	Used to hold new FQDN and aliases required once the server is moved.

Column name	Description
Notes	Free form text to provide any additional notes that may help during the move event

The above table is the basic information that is typically recorded in the tech info sheet. You should feel free to add columns for any information that engineers or analysts feel is critical to know during the move even. For example: a physical move should include additional information about the rack and elevation, NICs to Switches/Ports, HBA to SAN ports as well as other physical items changing.

A word of caution: if your teams feel they need additional information, ensure they are willing to gather, record and refer to it for each and every move. If information is only required for unique situations, you may want to use the notes section. A sheet with data in only a few entries spread across dozens of columns can be frustrating when individuals are unsure if the data is missing or not required. Rather than leave cells empty place "N/A" in the cell to indicate it was not required.

Move Method Options Example

The follow example demonstrates the idea behind documenting the chosen move methods for your datacenter migration. By developing a move method document, the project team is forced to think though, at a high-level the steps that go into each move option. This document should be developed through collaboration with the infrastructure teams.

This document is one of the best methods for starting the conversation with the infrastructure teams on how they see applications moving. As you collaborate with the infrastructure teams it is important to keep grounding the conversations with questions such as:

- How will this method affect the application analysts and customers?
- How will this method reduce the work load on the analyst and customers?
- How will this method give the application analysts and customers more control?
- What is the preferred move method from the infrastructure's perspective and what can the teams do to make that more appealing to the application analysts and customers?
- What if the method does not work for the application analyst or customer?

In this case, there were two destinations discussed and three methods. The document will depend on your datacenter move project requirements and should encompass all acceptable scenarios.

Although the move method document is intended to narrow the choices, the choice is ultimately made by the application owner. We often need to remind infrastructure teams to let go of the choice since the analysts ultimately owns the risk and responsibility for the move as well as the relationship with the customer.

Our experience with moving datacenters has demonstrated a key to success is to ensure the person most accountable for the outcome, owns the responsibility of make the decisions to get there. The infrastructure teams are accountable for supporting the move and providing the effective options, but the analysts and customer are accountable for the move's success.

Executive Summary

NewCo Group (NewCo) is closing its Boston campus which requires migrating applications and IT services in the Boston datacenter into the Portland datacenter (PDX) or Amazon cloud (AWS). Senior leadership has given the guidance of cloud first when choosing where an application will be relocated.

NewCo Group's systems, applications and data must be relocated from Boston with minimal down time while maintaining system integrity. The application migration activities represent most of the work and risk in most datacenter relocation programs.

In order to minimize the risk and standardize the work as much as possible, the datacenter migration program is establishing a standard application migration approach. This best practice approach takes advantage of technology capabilities, minimizes variation and accounts for individual application needs.

The standard allows teams to select from the following approaches to migrate their systems and applications:

- Virtual to Virtual Relocation
- Build New
- Physical Relocation

Within this standards document, each of the approaches is laid out along with the associated levels of risk, effort and typical outages so that teams may choose the most appropriate approach for their application. As each team prepares for their application migration, they will develop a build sheet[8] and cut sheet[9] that corresponds to the specifics of their application relocation following one of the standard migration approaches.

One of the greatest risks to successfully relocating applications is the addition of elective change. In order to reduce the risk introduced by change, the standard aims to avoid elective changes during the migration event. Elective changes to be avoided include changes to: platforms, configurations, operating systems, software, firmware and bios including version upgrades, patches or settings. The goal is to limit change to items that have been thoroughly tested prior to the migration event.

While a datacenter migration is one of the most complex programs any organization can undertake, following the guidelines in this application

---

[8]   Build Sheet – a detailed document defining the scope of an application or system to be migrated. This scope includes hardware, software, data and system interfaces. The build sheet describes the current state of what is to be migrated.

[9]   Cut Sheet – a detailed document defining the tasks to execute leading up to and during the application migration event. The level of detail during the migration event is at a minute by minute level of who is performing what and when, in order to avoid any confusion or mistakes that could lead to unplanned outages. A rollback plan is contained in the cut sheet along with its trigger point. The cut sheet describes how the migration will occur.

migration standard approach document will significantly reduce NewCo Group's risk, standardize the work and add predictability to the outcome of each application migration.

High-Level Approach

The Boston datacenter located on the Franklin campus is populated with a variety of physical hardware including:

- Networking components.
- Storage frames and disk.
- x86 servers.
- Mid-range computers.
- Backup.
- Phone systems (VoIP).
- UPS (uninterruptable power supplies).
- PDUs (power distribution unit).
- Server cabinets.
- Miles of copper, fiber and power cables.

Moving from one datacenter to another datacenter is an activity that most organizations seldom perform. A datacenter move is complex and expensive in relation to other technology projects an organization will take on, regardless of how the move is accomplished.

Most of the complexity involved in moving from one datacenter to another arises from the applications, middle ware and data that is running and stored on the different hardware components. The unique combination of hardware, software and data working to achieve a common purpose creates a system. It is the system that must be addressed in moving from one datacenter to another. When evaluating systems in the context of a move, it is helpful to divide them into business systems and shared systems.

Business systems are categorized as a group of diverse, but interdependent applications and their resources that interact to accomplish specific business functions. Examples of business systems include: PLM, MARC Fusion, and EDI. To meet business needs, NewCo has built their own business systems and have modified commercial off the shelf (COTS) packages creating a unique environment within Boston.

Shared systems are categorized as the group of application and their resources that provide common services. These common services may work standalone or support other systems in accomplishing specific business functions. Examples of shared systems include Email (MS Exchange), Active Directory (AD), DNS (IPAM), printing services, databases, security controls, VPN access and FTP. NewCo has deployed many shared systems, each with unique setting changes.

By identifying systems in this manner, systems engineers, analysts and application developers can evaluate the boundaries and interactions of each system. In very few cases do systems operate autonomously. This system to system interaction is what increases the complexity and risk of moving. While some systems may have high interaction with another business or shared system, that relationship may not be critical. Other systems may have a low interaction rate, but the success of the business transaction is heavily dependent on the other system's service. In many cases throughout NewCo the system to system interactions, criticality, timing and impacts are undocumented with some interactions unknown.

Understanding the systems' interactions is critical to unraveling the complexity, reducing the risk of unplanned outages and ensuring the systems operate correctly in the new datacenter.

At a macro level, NewCo will be moving systems out of Boston using an individual relocation approach (micro move) rather than a big bang approach in which all systems are moved at once. Individualized system moves are based on each system's requirements and interrelationships. Each system is decomposed into its components identifying interfaces, dependencies, job schedules, criticality, platforms and relationships. This decomposition allows the most appropriate relocation method to be employed at the individual component level. The goal is to match the requirements and risk to the move method and take advantage of technologies to reduce outage risk.

There are two primary[10] relocation destinations available. Those destinations are Amazon's cloud (AWS) environment and NewCo' Portland datacenter. Each location has certain migration methods available. Application analysts in collaboration with business users and this program's leadership will determine an application's destination and the most appropriate migration method. The application analyst bears responsibility and is the ultimate decision maker for the application's final destination and migration method.

Amazon Cloud

In order to follow senior leadership's guidance of cloud first the program will provide a cloud readiness assessment by application to analysts. The assessment considers application complexity, user community, server details, KPIs and integration requirements to make a recommendation on an application's compatibility for migrating to the cloud (AWS). This assessment is being performed by TBR Group, who provided the same level of assessment

---

[10] Business or shared systems may have specific requirements to relocate to another location. In general, this is the exception and must be negotiated with the program leadership on a case by case basis.

for the Texas datacenter applications. The results of the assessment will be available February 2017.

Because of the differences in computing, storage and networking services in AWS, applications migrating to AWS must be built new on servers in AWS' environment. Data must be copied up into AWS' storage. Network and security settings must be built new. The infrastructure team can provide the servers and assist in copying the data as well as building appropriate connections and firewall rules. Application analyst must provide the system to system and user connectivity as well as build the application and test its functionality in AWS.

Portland Datacenter

At a macro level, NewCo will be moving systems from Boston to PDX using an individual relocation approach rather than a big bang approach in which all systems are moved at once or large groups. Individualized system moves are based on each system's requirements and interrelationships. Each system is decomposed into its components identifying interfaces, dependencies, job schedules, criticality, platforms and relationships. This decomposition allows the most appropriate relocation method to be employed at the individual system level. The goal is to match the requirements and risk to the move method and take advantage of technologies to reduce outage risk. Within the individualized system move to PDX, several relocation methods are available including:

1. Virtual to Virtual Relocation (V2V)
2. Build New
3. Physical Relocation[11]

Multiple move methods may be utilized within a single system in order to meet the overall goals and system constraints. For example, a system may use a build new method for its web applications and databases along with a V2V method for its application level hosts.

This individualized approach to moving a datacenter is more finesse oriented since it moves components of the datacenter in micro move events designed to minimize impacts to end users of the systems. Additionally, breaking up the migration into smaller move events allows for these events to be stacked according to system requirements, criticality, business changes and resource availability. The micro move events are not serial; typically, several systems are moving in parallel throughout a structured move.

---

[11] Physical relocation is the least preferred. In general, this is the exception and must be negotiated with the program leadership on a case by case basis.

At a high-level the following table presents the pros, cons and assumptions of for the individualized approach.

Approach	Pros	Cons	Assumptions
Individualize the system moves	• Ability to match risk and outage duration to system capability and business constraints. • Detailed system knowledge is captured and documented for ongoing operations. • Greater ability to maintain SLAs. • Greater ability to minimize unplanned outages. • Takes advantage of hardware platform redundancies and high-availability. • Provides more flexibility to respond to changing business requirements and schedules. • Greater ability to test prior to move event. • Debug effort is contained to smaller number of components and changes. • Allows for resource management.	• New equipment is required. • Longer project duration than a big bang approach. • Higher NewCo system knowledge required. • Greater planning details required.	• NewCo staff levels on both the application and infrastructure teams are adequate to create detailed plans. • New equipment is available as required. • System migrations can be executed in phases. • Network bandwidth between Boston, PDX and AWS is adequate to support migrations and allow data / system communication across locations.

Constraints

With any project there are some constraints that must be managed. In the datacenter migration program there are two significant constraints that affect the systems migrating from Boston. Those constraints are:

- Staff reductions are set for March 31, 2017. Some of the staff reductions include individuals with critical knowledge of applications to be moved from Boston. Applications with staff reduction constraints will be moved first. Because of timing constraints, these applications will be moved to PDX in order to minimize complexity and reduce elective changes during the move. The affected applications are:
    - ELI
    - PLD
    - design Upload
    - ECOM, Business Objects
    - MicroStrategy
    - File Tracker / Real Estate
    - QuickBooks
- Senior leadership has established a cloud first strategy. This strategy presents risk for analysts and infrastructure teams which have not migrated or maintained systems in AWS. While the infrastructure team can provide support, ultimately the application analyst must be accountable for selecting the destination (PDX or AWS). Inputs into this decision will include the TBR Group application readiness assessment, business risk, time frame and complexity.
- Due to technical and business constraints, some applications may need to be migrated from Boston into a location other than PDX or AWS. All efforts should be made to avoid migrating to other locations and must be addressed on an exception basis.

While these constraints add some complexity, the build and cut sheets will consider the changes imposed by the constraints as systems migrate from Boston to their destination.

Individualized Systems Migration Discussion

Underlying the migration details are a few basic tenets that greatly increase the chance of success. These tenets are:

- Minimize change during the move process. Avoid changes to configurations, operating systems, software, firmware and bios including version upgrades, patches or settings. Only accept changes which have been thoroughly tested.
- Develop a detailed set of tasks to be executed for each system and its underlying components. These details are documented in the build sheet and cut sheet for each system.

- Involve the stakeholders who have day to day responsibility for the use and administration of the system in the planning and execution phases of the move.

Moving systems from one location to another can take on several forms when applied at a system or sub-system level. To better understand the advantages of an individualized system migration approach, the following discussion breaks down the activities and presents additional detail for the various options when individually applied at a system level.

Virtual to Virtual Relocation

Relocating virtual servers and data is referred to as a Virtual to Virtual Relocation (V2V). A V2V relocation utilizes the tools available from the virtual environment software manufacturer (or third party) to move virtual servers and data.

The virtual server can only exist in one location at time. No testing can be done prior to executing the move. Since a V2V relocation is a bit for bit copy from one location to another the server, application and its data in PDX will be identical to its last state in Boston datacenter.

The steps involved include:

1. A VMware based compute environment exists in PDX and will be available to receive virtually relocated guests[12].
   a. Ensure virtual environment capacity on the equipment and maintain operational support.
   b. Test the communication between virtual environments in Boston and PDX.
   c. Extend connectivity from the virtual environment in Boston to the virtual environment in PDX.
2. Utilize the virtual environment's tools to move the virtual servers across to the new location.
   a. Start the copy host and data from Boston's virtual environment to PDX's virtual environment.
   b. Allow data synchronization to maintain data and application parity until move event. This is non-intrusive and occurs over several days in the background while the server in Boston remains active.
   c. Stop Boston virtual server, allow final data synchronization to complete.
   d. Validate server running on PDX virtual environment (IP address and host name will be changing).

---

[12] In a virtual compute environment, the virtual servers are referred to as guests.

       e. Update any application configurations affected by the new IP address and host name.

       f. Using host file point to PDX virtual server and smoke test application.

3. Change DNS (IPAM) to point to the host located in PDX.
4. Validate application, interfaces and user access.
5. After the virtual servers have been migrated to the new location, tested and approved, the virtual server(s) in Boston will be decommissioned.

Moving applications and data using a V2V method is straightforward and represents low-risk, repeatable option. This assumes the systems are virtualized and stable in Boston prior to executing a V2V migration. The nature of the V2V relocation dictates that no changes will occur during the relocation process.

Rating	Risk	Documentation level	Outage time
High (10)			
Medium (5)			
Low (1)	X	X	X

Risk: A V2V relocation does not allow testing prior to the migration event. Minimal risk is involved since the virtual environment tools were designed to perform the movement of virtual servers with minimal disruption of service. Services can be brought back on-line in the Boston virtual environment if an issue arises during the migration providing a solid fall back plan. Equipment for the virtual environment is pre-staged and tested prior to migration reducing issues.

Documentation: Documentation is required to ensure steps are identified for using the virtual tools to complete a successful cut over and test the system in the new virtual environment. The same documented steps will be repeated for each virtual server, reducing the overall documentation effort required. Application specific testing and communication documentation (cut sheet) remains a requirement for this type of relocation.

Outage time: A V2V migration can occur with minimal outage time when planned correctly. Utilizing the virtual environment tools correctly for migrating systems is key to minimizing planned service outages during the system migration.

Build New

Build new is the only option for systems moving to AWS. It is also an option for systems moving to PDX. A build new relocation migrates the application and data without physically moving hardware or virtual servers. Instead new or repurposed equipment (or virtual servers) is set up, a new version of the application is installed, and the data is ported over electronically. A build new involves:

1. Installing new or repurposed equipment in the new location.
2. Installing the operating system and application on the new physical equipment or virtual servers.
3. Testing the new equipment and applications for functionality.
4. Copying all relevant data and keeping it in synch with the current data source.
5. Install, configure and pre-production testing of the application.
6. Stopping the application at source location.
7. Synchronizing the last set of data.
8. Production testing the functionally.
9. Pointing production to the new location.

This is the same process used for most application upgrades onto new hardware or virtual servers. Planning this method of moving applications and data separate from the equipment they are installed on, is relativity straightforward and represents a low risk.

Rating	Risk	Documentation level	Outage time
High (10)			
Medium (5)		X	
Low (1)	X		X

A build new relocation is appropriate for systems running on physical equipment with very little down time availability. This approach requires equipment/virtual servers to be established in PDX for the system to be installed new. The equipment vacated in the move may be placed into the pool of equipment which will become seed equipment for the next system. All other elective changes to applications running on servers should be avoided.

All elective changes should be avoided in order to reduce risk introduced through change. An application, database or OS upgrade raises the schedule and complexity risk from low to medium.

Risk: The risk, without an upgrade, in this method is reduced by the fact that the original system can be brought back on-line if an issue arises during the cut over providing a solid fall back plan. Equipment (or virtual server) is pre-staged and tested prior to migration. A poorly documented detail move plan and lack of understanding how the application and data interact represents a potential for error to occur during the migration. The other area of risk is in the attempt to upgrade the new system during the move. A build new approach for moving systems from one set of equipment to another should be between "like for like" equipment to minimize potential errors. Additional pre-migration testing of the system should be performed to ensure complete functionality. These same tests should be repeated post migration.

Elective changes should be avoided at all costs.

Documentation Level: Detailed documentation is required to ensure a successful cut over. The cut over typically involves several networking, security and storage changes to occur in order to direct communication appropriately to the system's new location.

Outage time: The amount of outage time can vary significantly. Data requires a final synchronization across the network to the PDX datacenter before it can be put back into production. Testing time of component functionality also influences the outage duration. More complex components require longer testing times.

Physical Relocation:

NewCo should have a minimal number of physical relocations. However, if the system is a viable candidate for a physical relocation, the following standard applies regardless of platform.

A physical relocation involves:

1. Shut off the application.
2. Change the IP address and ports to match the new PDX configuration.
3. Shut equipment off.
4. Un-cabling the equipment.
5. Pulling the equipment out of the rack.
6. Packaging the equipment.
7. Transport equipment to the new location.
8. Un-packaging the equipment.
9. Place equipment into the correct new rack location.
10. Cable the equipment correctly.
11. Turn on the correct ports.
12. Test the system.

With careful planning and documentation this method of moving applications or data along with the equipment it is installed on is relativity straightforward and may represent a low-cost option when applied at the micro-level.

Rating	Risk	Documentation level	Outage time
High			X
Medium	X		
Low		X	

A physical relocation strategy is most appropriate for systems which can accept significant downtime or are highly redundant. A physical relocation strategy is also used for non-critical or non-redundant components of a larger system in which at least 72 hours of downtime for executing the move is acceptable.

Risk: This option carries a moderate amount of risk if the installation documentation is incomplete since fall back options are limited in nature. Risks include: equipment damage in transit, incorrect assembly into the new PDX rack, operating systems fail to reboot, incorrect IP address or port configuration changes. Issues encountered with this relocation method require working through one at a time serially. If a system with a large number of components is moved physically at one time, even for simple issues the resolution complexity grows exponentially.

Older equipment involved in a physical move runs a higher risk of drive failures. Backups, spare drives and recovery plans should be part of move plan for older equipment. In many cases changing the approach to a build new approach will be the most prudent risk mitigation.

Documentation level: The documentation requirement for a physical move is focused on the physical aspects of the equipment including ports, cables, interface cards, locations and installation instructions. The documentation should also contain the software, software license information and data contents of the equipment to ensure complete understanding of turning the equipment off and back on in the correct order.

Outage: In a non-redundant environment the system outage duration needs to consider:

- How many pieces of equipment will be migrated in one move event.
- How many hands will be involved (technical staff and freighters).
- Time requirement to backup and shut down applications, databases, operating systems and equipment.
- Logistics for loading docks, elevators, hallways, dollies, packaging.
- Physical time to disassemble, crate, uncrate and reassemble based on class (a midrange requires more time than an x86 server).
- Outage durations estimates need to be validated prior to the move event.

In the case of highly redundant systems that can support the loss of a component without stopping the work flow, outage time is theoretically zero. In this case the risk is low, and the cost is minimal while the documentation level remains the same as in a non-redundant physical move. In the case of a highly redundant system the physical move is performed in stages so that the system can continue to support the work load by utilizing the remaining equipment while a manageable number of its components are physically moved.

Conclusion

NewCo has approximately 60 applications and services that are provided from the Boston raised floor. Rather than dictate a single approach for all application migration, NewCo will use an individualized approach for each application base on its requirements and platform needs.

While the choice of relocation method will be up to the application teams to agree on as they develop their relocation plans, all relocations will follow standard operating procedures (SOP) of the Boston datacenter migration program. Those SOPs include:

- Creation of a "Build Sheet".
- Creation of a "Cut Sheet".
- Follow NewCo change control procedures.
- Avoid elective changes during the migration event.

Any systems which do not fit into the planned relocation option standards or cannot adhere to the projects SOPs will need exception approval from the program's leadership.

Appendix

Application Scope Boundaries

Business applications are categorized based on the expected disposition at the end of the project. These dispositions include:

- Migration from Boston to AWS
- Migration from Boston to PDX
- Sunset (or Retire) & Decommission in Boston

This list may not include all shared systems to be migrated such as: Active Directory, Lync, Exchange. Some applications have been tagged for decommission but final disposition remains to be verified.

PLD	design Upload	Access DB Server
ECOM	ELI	Business Objects
MicroStrategy	File Tracker / Real Estate	QuickBooks
MARQIN	TIBCO	Security
DLP PCI_CSS Scan	SIEM	MARC Fusion
Kronos (PLS)	File Maker	Master Calendar (PLS)
SATRASystems	Adobe AEM	Loftware
GetPaid	TaxWare Server (SAP)	Market IT FTP Server
Market IT Script Server	SPEEDI	WASDAT - Retail
HotSpotlink (Retail)	Retail Remoteware	Retail Systems
SFA	US Retail File Server	NDDigital – Modo Am
HR - PEX Tool	E-Invoice Server - Rubicon	E-Invoice Server - Moab
GMMT	Elastic Search	Blue License server
FrontRunner Team Licensing	CAMP Archive Files	SolidWorks
CCure 9000	ReConnet	SAP Interface
Hitachi Command Center (Infra)	Avaya Telephony	Innovation Pyramid
LogicMonitor	UTC Font Server	SCCM - EUC
End User Monitoring	TMG	AM.newco.biz
Domain Controller	Domain Controller	NewCoINT

Risk Analysis Background

The nature of moving systems from one datacenter to another involves risk.

In order to establish a risk comparison between alternatives, the following items were identified to represent NewCo' risk at a macro-level for moving from Boston:

- The AWS environment is relatively new to NewCo. Few NewCo applications have been migrated to AWS. There are two major areas of risk:
  - Risks associated with the migration onto native AWS services are different than those in Boston or PDX.
  - Operational and application support processes will change and have not been fully tested
- Re-assembly of equipment failures caused by incorrect or misreading documentation.
- Outage windows exceed customers' service level agreements (SLA) and requirements.
- Equipment damaged or lost on route.
- Systems fail to operate correctly after installation in the PDX datacenter or AWS.
- Network or storage communication failures.
- IP Address conflicts prevent communications to and from the application or systems after moving to the PDX datacenter or AWS.
- System interface communication failures.
- Unaccounted for or unknown system attributes.
- AWS security requirements are undocumented and unknown at this time

The risks associated with moving individual systems are typically mitigated by isolating the move to a single or small number of system components at one time known as a micro move event. The change which translates into risk, involved over multiple small move events can be more tightly managed.

Assumptions

Assumptions can represent a significant risk if all stakeholders do not agree with the assumptions. In order to predict needs and outcomes of alternative move methods, several assumptions have been made. The following assumptions have been used as inputs into the process:

1. The individualized migration method approach will use multiple methods for a complete system to take advantage of equipment redundancy
2. The existing network in PDX and AWS allows communication with all equipment, systems and applications in Boston.
3. The existing network in Boston can communicate with all equipment, systems and applications in PDX and AWS.
4. There may be a need to modify user access policies to allow external users to access apps in PDX or AWS

5. Systems will receive new IP addresses, host names and VLAN assignments in PDX and AWS.
6. System change will be minimized during the move. Changes to configurations, operating systems, software, firmware and bios including version upgrades, patch or settings will be avoided during the migration event.
7. Systems will be tested, and results documented prior to the move creating a baseline. Following the move tests will be repeated and the results compared to the baseline validating system quality.
8. Data backups will be taken prior to the move as appropriate.
9. All equipment involved in physical relocations will be wrapped in static free wrap and packaged to provide appropriate protection during relocation.
10. A crate and freight company will un-rack, package, relocate, rack and re-cable the equipment.
11. NewCo will shut down and restart all equipment as well as diagram out all cable connections.
12. Detailed move plans will identify the steps necessary to migrate systems using build sheets and cut sheets. The plans will have enough detail for someone other than the author to execute the plan.
13. Outage windows for the move which are longer than standard maintenance windows will be negotiated with NewCo customers.
14. Unplanned outage is defined as a duration in which the system is off-line that exceeds a negotiated move duration (change window) and did not receive a customer approved extension.
15. Sufficient staff and resources are available for the move regardless of method.
16. Availability and engagement from technical teams in technical assessment/reviews, sprint execution, cutover activities.

Beyond Traditional Waterfall Project Management

Over the years many of our clients have adopted our framework to manage their other complex infrastructure projects. The reason our framework works well is that although on the surface it may appear different, all the fundamentals of project management are there.

If we compare the ROPE framework to traditional project management, the similarities and differences become apparent.

Item	Framework	Waterfall Project Management
Project Charter	Follows PMO requirements for project initiation	Follows PMO requirements for project initiation
Scope	Project charter scope statement Move matrix – One row for each item/deliverable, it's due date and individual responsible. Timestamp provides date each item was added, deleted or changed	Project charter scope statement
Requirements	Build sheet maintains the requirements, boundaries and interfaces for each item in the move matrix Build sheet master rolls all build sheet requirements together in order to reveal larger system dependencies Changes are made as required to the individual build sheet in order to maintain their accuracy and automatically rolled up Tech info reflects configuration change requirements for individual applications tied back to build sheets	Separate requirements document is created for the project Requirements are considered frozen after design activities Changes are discouraged and costly Requirements do not always tie to elements of the schedule

Item	Framework	Waterfall Project Management
	Cut sheet tasks reflect timing, communication, and deployment requirements tied back to move matrix, build sheet and tech info sheet	
WBS	Move matrix maintains a list of all deliverables Cut sheet maintains work required to produce each deliverable at a detailed level Moves decisions closer to the work	Separate WBS document
Schedule	Move matrix maintains overall schedule for individual deliverable items, their current status and assigned to resource Cut sheet provides detailed scheduling plan for producing each deliverable Activities are decoupled as much as possible allowing independence of deployment Delivers increasing, incremental value to the business	Detailed, long-term project schedule with single timeline Fully completed product delivered at the end of the timeline Linear-phased approach creates dependencies
Budget	A budget template for estimating and tracking budget and actual spend is provided. The budget template is tied to the dashboard for real-time transparency of planned and actual project spending.	Follows PMO requirements for project. Reporting is a separate activity.

Item	Framework	Waterfall Project Management
Change control	Driven by guiding principles Managed through program tower leads, escalated to advisory board and steering board Moves decisions closer to the work	Change control required to maintain scope at governance level. Assumption of frozen requirements upon completing design phase Changes in deliverables are discouraged and costly
Risk management	RAIDq used to manage risks and provide visibility to senior leadership through the dashboard	Risks managed in a separate document and reported separately
Stakeholder involvement	Moves the work and its decisions to the individual most capable of completing it Stakeholders are involved throughout the framework as participants in the process Realtime visibility to project information is available on the dashboard to all stakeholders Multiple communications via multiple methods are used to inform impacted stakeholders prior to events	Stakeholders typically involved in the beginning and end of the project Visibility is provided through status reports Typically, standard organizational process is relied on to communicate events

Large complex infrastructure projects are inherently filled with ambiguity and risk. Just as a long journey is taken one step at a time, applying the principles of the ROPE framework brings order to chaos by stepping through the project and delivering incremental successes that build increasing customer value.

The ROPE framework is designed to be flexible, building on the foundation of agile, lean and scrum methodologies embracing similar principles. Those principles are:

- Direct interactions between individuals is more powerful at problem solving and completing work than processes and tools.

170

- Success is achieved by teams working together not comprehensive documentation.
- Customer collaboration permits work to flow within the rhythm of the business.
- Adapting to change is more important than blindly adhering to a failed plan.
- Governance is achieved through transparency and not command and control.
- Work is only helpful if it improves overall throughput of quality deliverables.

By applying these concepts and principles an organization can successfully move a datacenter or complete any complex infrastructure project.

www.ingramcontent.com/pod-product-compliance
Lightning Source LLC
Chambersburg PA
CBHW080010210526
45170CB00015B/1968